Richard Travers Smith

Man's Knowledge of Man and of God

Six discourses delivered before the University of Dublin at the Donellan lecture,

1884-5

Richard Travers Smith

Man's Knowledge of Man and of God
Six discourses delivered before the University of Dublin at the Donellan lecture, 1884-5

ISBN/EAN: 9783337219628

Printed in Europe, USA, Canada, Australia, Japan

Cover: Foto ©Thomas Meinert / pixelio.de

More available books at **www.hansebooks.com**

MAN'S KNOWLEDGE

OF

MAN AND OF GOD

SIX DISCOURSES

*DELIVERED BEFORE THE UNIVERSITY OF DUBLIN
AT THE DONELLAN LECTURE, 1884-5*

BY

RICHARD TRAVERS SMITH, D.D.

Vicar of S. Bartholomew's, and Canon of S. Patrick's, Dublin

London

MACMILLAN AND CO.

AND NEW YORK

1886

PREFACE.

THESE lectures had been prepared for the press before I became acquainted with Lotze's *Microcosmus;* otherwise they would have contained many confirmations drawn from that admirable work. But in the last lecture I should have urged that the views of the nature of God, upon which the Christian Church has worked, are of a less speculative character than Lotze (bk. viii. ch. 4) seems to allow, and partake rather of that close connection with every-day thinking and living which this great writer vindicates for religion in general, and specially for Christianity.

Many will turn from the subject of these pages as metaphysical. There are really no metaphysics properly so called in the volume. Ontology, or the science of being, is not touched; only attention is directed to our ordinary experience of the working of our minds in individual life and mutual intercourse. I am well aware that reflection even upon the commonest matters of experience assumes an abstract and difficult character by the very fact that it is reflection, and more so when literary skill is wanting. But whatever be the measure of my own success, I have no doubt of the importance of my subject. In the great controversy upon belief, all discussions of history, science, and doctrine are but subsidiary to the cardinal question whether the faith offered us is such as we are forced to want and fitted to receive. Changes of faith, one way or other, which seem to be decided by learned argument, are really ruled by men's personal inward impulse. But the truest test to decide whether a faith is adapted to our necessary wants is furnished by the inquiry whether it falls in with those beliefs which are obviously and necessarily required in daily life. That faith will stand which best answers this test when morally and thoughtfully applied, with those aids from within and without which life teaches us to use for distinguishing transitory opinions and inclinations from real necessities of the mind and soul.

CONTENTS.

INTRODUCTION 1

II.
SELF-KNOWLEDGE 51

III.
KNOWLEDGE OF MEN 92

IV.
WE KNOW GOD THROUGH SELF-KNOWLEDGE 131

V.
WE KNOW GOD IN NATURE AND MAN 173

VI.
GOD REVEALED 216

MAN'S KNOWLEDGE

OF

MAN AND OF GOD.

INTRODUCTION.

"The invisible things of God are clearly seen, being understood by the things that are made."—ROM. i. 20.

"Who knoweth the spirit of man that goeth upward, and the spirit of the beast that goeth downward to the earth?"—ECCL. iii. 21.

1. WE are about to maintain that we know God in the same way as we know man. It is an argument from analogy, and seeks to recommend religion by reason of its agreement with the experience of life. This kind of argument has been a weapon in the hands of Christians since long before the time of Butler, and its value is greater now than ever before. For natural knowledge has become so extensive and

Power of the argument which depends upon the analogy between religion and natural knowledge.

so valuable that religion has, with most of us, little chance of acceptance unless it comes recommended by it. The progress of natural knowledge has resembled that of certain empires, which after having for a long time existed by the forbearance of more powerful states, have come to be the arbiters of the political world, and decide whether those very kingdoms shall be allowed to live, and what their boundaries shall be. Accordingly the most popular book which for many years has appeared upon the religious question has been one which claims to show that natural law rules in the spiritual world; and that between religion and nature there exists not merely analogy but continuity, the one being the further application of the powers and principles which prevail in the other.

It is not difficult to see why this argument possesses so much force. On the one hand, if we are permitted to assume the being of a God we have then in the facts of our earthly life specimens of His action and indications of the laws which prevail in His government, and good reason is thereby given for holding that He will make further applications of the same principles. But it must not be supposed that reasoning from analogy loses all its force if the being of God is regarded as something to be proved, not assumed, or even as something not true. In that case the conditions and surroundings of our earthly lives, and the corresponding bent and habits of the human mind, remain as facts however they have come about. And if it can be shown that they are such as point to religion, then a religion must be provided, unless man is to be left without the supply of an essential want. Under these circumstances some men will draw from the existence of wants for which there is no earthly provision, the conclusion that human life is full of miserable illusion; some will attempt the creation of a religion without a God; while some will hold that such an education of man suffices to prove the existence of a God to carry it on. But all will acknowledge the power of the argument.

A great part of the force which the argument from analogy possesses is due to the fact that when well handled it is more than a mere argument; that is, it is not a mere piece of reasoning addressed to our intellects, but receives constant aid from our sympathetic interest in the views which it gives of human life. Our affections and our moral nature are enlisted as the laws which rule them in daily life are vividly set before us; and the interest is carried forward into that larger sphere which religion offers them. A better instance of this cannot be found than certain of our Saviour's parables. In many of these the Lord not only uses earthly things as illustrations of heavenly, but founds an argument upon the analogy between the two. As for instance, "How much more shall your Father which is in heaven give good things to them that ask Him:" and "How much more shall your heavenly Father do also unto you if ye from your hearts forgive not every one his brother their trespasses!" We have here a piece of reasoning of great power depending upon the analogy between the principles which rule human nature and those which must govern Him who has framed human nature so. Yet the reasoning is not addressed to the bare intellect, but also to our human affections and our human sense of justice, which come to the aid of the argument as we recognise the picture of fatherly love and the just demand for punishment upon the cruel and unforgiving.

The "how much more" of our Lord's argument suggests another practical power which reasoning from analogy possesses. It may sometimes assume with great force and justice the form of an argument *a fortiori*. It may appeal not merely to what we know of the laws which prevail in this life as affording reason for supposing that they prevail beyond this life. But it may point to the defects in their working here as giving hope of a better and more complete operation hereafter. If it can do this with truth it may depend upon a vast amount of help from man's emotional nature, which struggles against the troubles and imperfections of his earthly conditions almost as much as it apprehends their happiness, and is still more easily roused to hope for what he misses here than to fear the loss of what he has. To be sure this use of the analogy between things human and divine is liable to just suspicion. It may easily lose its grasp upon analogy altogether and wander off into hopes and beliefs which are recommended not by their agreement with experienced facts but by their contrast with them. Yet very truthful and thoughtful people have often felt justified in believing that in the further applications of natural law, for which the spiritual and the future world give room, explanations may be found of many difficulties and defects which oppress us as we observe their present operation. So that one who accepts nature and not religion may be like a man who invests his means in securities which bring him much immediate loss, and sells out just at the point where without further expenditure he would have largely gained by leaving his money where it was.

2. We have just said that feeling and conscience are proper helps to the intellect in apprehending religious truth. But when we compare religious truths with earthly, the conviction is forced upon us that feeling and conscience are more than mere helps to logic in finding truth. They are themselves organs for the discovery of truth. So far from needing to be chary as to the formal logic of our argument, we see that the more formal it is the less it is like life. "Il est," says Joubert, "de très graves matières et des questions fort importantes où les idées decisives doivent venir des sentiments: si elles viennent d'ailleurs tout se perdra. Penser ce que l'on ne

Now natural knowledge comes not merely through the intellect, but through the feelings.

sent pas, c'est mentir à soi-même. Tout ce qu'on pense it faut le penser avec son être tout entier, âme et corps."[1] This must be taken careful account of if analogy is to be used aright. Let us notice in a little detail how the matter stands.

In life we are all agreed that the understanding must not be left at the mercy of the feelings or even of the moral impulses, which if allowed to work unchecked become a kind of higher sensuality. There ought to be harmony and union between conviction and emotion. The inward man should advance like a disciplined army: the solid mass of intellectual belief supported by the lighter squadrons of feeling, which in their turn depend on it and cannot be safely thrown forward by themselves. But this does not impose on us in the affairs of life a fixed sequence by which logical convictions must be first acquired, and the feelings duly admitted when their time comes, moderated in their behaviour by the strict demands of logical demonstration.

On the contrary, we find by experience that

[1] Joubert, *Pensées*, vol. ii. pp. 123, 124.

the first response which our organism makes to the presence of facts, either true or imagined to be true, is made in the form of feeling, not of knowledge. The presence of external facts in the time of childhood causes feeling and action in us long before we can be said to know; unless knowledge be taken in a sense which has in it more of instinct or impulse than of intellectual conviction.

3. Moreover, when in after years we interrogate ourselves as to the precise nature of the facts which roused our feeling in those times of instinct, we often find ourselves perplexed in answering. And even in the maturity of our powers, though we acknowledge the anomaly of feeling without knowledge to justify it, yet complete inability to resist feeling and even an absolute conviction that it is right feeling may be accompanied by the greatest difficulty in representing to the mind the facts on which it is founded. And when, with the utmost exertion of thought, we attempt to put the reasons of our feeling into form, either for our own satisfaction or for that of others, we generally find that our justi-

And the intellect has great difficulty in representing to itself the message of the feelings.

fication loses nearly all its force in the process of stating it. We find that there is room for varying judgments upon it, and that there is something in it which cannot be presented for judgment at all. It must be allowed that in our natural life feeling has always its part with thought in guiding us to truth, and that if the guidance of feeling be imperfect that of thought is the same.

Nay, it might be plausibly maintained that feeling goes generally right except where thought leads it astray. Feeling stands in more direct relation to our surroundings than thought. And it is only by taking account of the information which feelings convey that thought can give its verdicts. For instance, bodily feelings alone convey to us the presence of material objects external to us. Understanding receives and combines their messages in wonderful ways. But when bodily sensations cease to be actually present, as when we have seen something for a moment, or pushed against something in the dark, and understanding is left by a process of sheer reflection to tell what the true message and meaning of the sensation was, we

constantly find it at fault. It cannot recall the sensation with sufficient distinctness, and often persuades itself that something was seen or felt which was not, or that something really felt was only imagined. And even when the sensation is not of such a passing nature, still, if the mind takes up a wrong impression with persistence, or even assumes persistently an attitude of reflection and of questioning, it will be often able to pervert the true meaning of a sensation even in its very presence. Many a white stone has been taken for a ghost by persons predisposed that way; and many a preoccupied man gazes upon his dinner or upon his book without thinking of putting them to their proper use. For reflection is so different an attitude from sensation, that it is capable of shutting our senses against the messages of the external world, or our minds against the messages of the senses. Thus savages, whose minds have not assumed so persistent an attitude of reflection as those of civilised men, are known to be truer observers of external things.

To be sure, if the word truth be so defined as to designate intellectual convictions alone, it goes without saying that the intellect is the only guide to truth. But truth may more usefully be taken to mean external reality than to denote any theories of our minds. And in this better sense of the word truth our possession of it consists in a certain harmony of relation not only of our intellect but of our whole nature towards the reality amid which we live. Truth possessed by the intellect alone may be a useless and dormant piece of property even if it can be said to be possessed at all. But a fruitful possession of truth is a more complex matter. It consists first in feeling true impressions and then in reproducing these for the mind in their true form and force, and then in deducing from this record a conviction which shall provide for the continuance and for the due growth of the feelings as circumstances demand.

4. For an entire inability to support feeling by a definite belief, or even a neglect to make the attempt, though an imperfect one, may be followed by disastrous results to feeling itself. Some one by assailing our inadequate thoughts may miserably disturb, or even destroy, many good and true feelings which were connected with them,

<small>But the feelings require for their support that the mind shall observe and record their message.</small>

just as a member of some commercial house who has done his own share of business in an admirable manner, finds himself ruined by his connection with an incapable or indolent partner.

A familiar instance of this in common life is found in our knowledge of the character of the people with whom we live. The truest discernment of character is made by instinctive feeling; or if it be an intellectual process it is one which is not conscious of itself. It grows through attractions and repulsions as natural as our desire or dislike of this or that food. The reason why, we cannot tell. And some steady natures to their great benefit frame these impressions into a mental conviction very difficult to shake. But there are others whom a novel theory regarding a friend's character may surprise into doubt if not into acquiescence. Their feelings, although they may have been true to real facts of the case, have never been sufficiently formulated into conviction. And when the new theory presents itself to the intellect it finds the ground unoccupied. The new theory has perhaps some appearances in its favour. It accounts for some of the facts of the case. Other supports are quickly added or imagined. A new set of feelings, the more violent because they are new, spring up to enforce the new belief. And the old impressions are for the time absent and forgotten. Such was the history of Othello's change of mind to Desdemona.

I meet a certain person for the first time. When we have parted I ask myself what is my judgment of his character. To make myself capable of answering the question I have to take care that my feelings and instincts have been in a candid condition and able to take an impression faithfully. And to answer it with any effect I have to recall my feelings during the interview as they really were; a difficult matter to do with truth. I have to compel my mind to make a proper deduction from the impressions without regard to the prejudices about human character in general, or this one in particular, of which it is sure to be full; and I must be on my guard against the common temptation of laying down a more exact theory than the facts warrant. To give a just judgment upon first impressions of character requires a peculiar quickness both of feeling and intellect and a peculiar balance between the two. Should the acquaintance continue and opportunity be given for a more deliberate judgment these conditions will still remain the same. It will still be necessary that the feelings should be healthy and active in taking in the meaning of every new fact we learn or observe: and that the understanding should not merely keep the feelings in check but give them a respectful attention. Seeing how ill-balanced the minds of men are in themselves it is no wonder that the conclusions to which they come about one another's characters are so very various.

5. To maintain that reality is found by powers other than the understanding is far from implying any depreciation of science or of the truths which it teaches. On the contrary, no one who takes the view now recognised by science of man's place in nature can be surprised to find feeling and reason mixing in mutual helpfulness or mutual antagonism in his guidance to truth. Man, like every other organism, is engaged in adjusting himself to his environment. In the lower creatures, to whose

Science does not teach us to regard the intellect as our only guide to truth.

nature that of man stands parallel, and even related, the adjustments between organism and environment are made through unconscious feeling without any reasoning. It is thus that even the plants seek and receive their sustenance and the wild beast finds its food and avoids its foes. Every feeling and instinct in the lower creatures is a kind of unconscious reply to the unconscious question "What is it that surrounds me?" To help him in answering this question man has understanding. But his understanding grows by gradual stages out of the instincts and feelings of the lower forms of creation. And while he has acquired this new help to adjustment, he has not left behind the lower helps of feeling and instinct. These remain beside his understanding as correspondences between his nature and his surroundings. What just claim then can the understanding make to be his sole guide to truth; his sole help in answering the question, What is it that surrounds me? And at what stage in his development could the understanding be supposed to have acquired such a right? Aristotle says that it is probable many improbable things will happen, and in like manner we may say that it is scientific to believe that a great deal of knowledge does not come by science. But this is often forgotten. The intellect sets out upon the task of registering experience and calls this science. But engrossed by its own methods it comes to deny reality to any experiences except its own, and to dictate to faculties which ought to have as real a share as it has in adjusting our relations to our surroundings.

6. If we are to expect that the reasons for religious belief will be the same as those for natural belief we must look for a similar mixture of feeling and understanding in the attainment of religious truth.

And this is as true in religion as is natural knowledge.

It is not so much conceded as imperatively demanded by our men of science, that the criteria of truth in religion shall be the same as those which we find applicable in natural life. The demand is perfectly just: therefore we must take care that we do not narrow our principle of analogy by regarding only that species of natural truth which may be described as scientific. There is an immense department of natural truth which does not come under this head: namely, all the intercourse of living beings with living beings. This intercourse may indeed be made the subject of scientific observations which may be registered for scientific knowledge. But the knowledge which is necessary for practical use in the intercourse itself is a different thing, and the two should by no means be confounded.

Now this practical natural knowledge which living beings acquire and use in their intercourse with each other is shown by any just observation to come through feelings, instincts, sentiments, or powers to which no name can be given at all. Why should it be different with religious knowledge? There is every reason why it should be the same with religion if religion is the intercourse of living beings on earth with living beings or a living being above nature. The constitution of man requires that this intercourse with a supernatural being shall take place, like that with natural beings, through impressions on the mind which indicate an external presence: such impressions as, in a general way, we call feelings. And as in intercourse with men, so also in that with God, there will be a difficulty on the part of the mind in observing or in recalling the true nature of the feelings and in stating rightly the true deduction from them. The feeling is one thing, the remembrance of it as reproduced and reflected on by the understanding is another. True impressions may be forgotten or falsified to the memory or even in their very presence, and a determined attitude of the mind may hinder the access of other similar impressions, or deny them if they come.[1]

The religious beliefs of men may be said to embody their judgment upon the character of the universe. And if the difficulties in maintaining the healthy action of feeling and understanding, each in its sphere, and the due balance of their relation to one another bring about the greatest variations both from the reality and from

---

[1] "How does it come to pass that in this branch of knowledge there are so many and so contrary systems? This strange phenomenon may I think be accounted for if we distinguish between consciousness and reflection, which are often improperly confounded. The first is common to all men at all times, but is insufficient of itself to give us clear and distinct notions of the operations of which we are conscious, and of their mutual relations and minute distinctions. The second—to wit, attentive reflection upon these operations, making them objects of thought, surveying them attentively on all sides—is so far from being common to all men that it is the lot of very few. The habit of this reflection, even in those whom nature has fitted for it, is not to be obtained without much pains and practice."—*Reid's Works, by Hamilton*, p. 433.

one another in men's judgments of human character, we may expect the same in their judgment of the character of the universe, that is to say in their religious belief. And the happy or disastrous results to their own character and happiness which flow from their judgments in religion meet no unfit parallel in the effects which result from truth or error in their appreciation of the people with whom they are brought in contact during life.

Let us observe how religion works in a man's life. Like every other subject on which the mind of man employs itself, religion implies feelings experienced by which a reality is recognised, and ideas in the mind resting on these experiences and in turn lending support to them. The idea common under different forms to every religion is that of a supernatural reality in contact with the soul. This supernatural reality has been almost universally held to be personal, by reason of the very nature of its contact with the personal soul. But even were it only the Eternal Not Ourselves, it must make its footing in man's nature good by means of felt experiences and the mental ideas in which past experiences are registered and future ones are sought for. Now it might be thought inconsistent with the immediate connection with the soul which religion, if true, must possess, that the intervention of other human beings should have much to do with suggesting both religious ideas and religious feelings; so much, that little of either would be developed if the training of the unformed mind were not taken possession of by teachers in a more or less deliberate way. Be it surprising or not, such is the fact. It is the fact not merely in religion, but in every other department of our experience. And our dependence upon other men is perhaps less surprising in religion than anywhere else, because religion, as its name implies, is an influence common to all, which binds men together and must be supposed to be intended by the spiritual power from which it proceeds to have this effect.

Teachers of religion are brought in their very earliest attempts face to face with the difficulty of securing a due balance of intellectual conception and spiritual feeling in those committed to their training. It is easy to rouse the religious emotions of children with great vehemence, while supplying them with mental conceptions so indefinite that they vanish as the mind becomes strong enough to demand its rights, or so ill-supported by proof that the first breath of doubt will overthrow them. It is easy, on the other hand, to make religion an affair of catechisms and Bible lessons learnt by rote; in which case it will have no support from the feelings, and it may really be a matter of no great moral importance whether a belief so purely theoretical is formally retained in after life or not.

What teacher is sufficient for these things? It is impossible by any amount of reflection to lay down rules for the training of the feelings and the understanding of children in due and equal measure. In devising such rules and trying to observe them, we should probably lose all the life and sympathy with our pupils which give power either over their hearts or minds. So that there seems to be no complete help for the present state of things, which commits the child's mind in matters of religion (as well as in all other matters) to a miscellaneous variety of influences, exercised by nurses, playfellows and chance companions, and that often in a more effective manner than parents and catechists can attain. This confused mass of motive and suggestion to feeling and to mind is the inheritance of an immense series of similar educations exercised upon the successive generations of humanity. "Whatever," to borrow Milton's expression, "time in his huge drag-net has brought down," this it is which composes the conglomerate of powers that influence every mind. And, as might be expected under such a state of things, the feelings are constantly led wrong and the understanding as constantly. The feelings cease not to misguide the understanding and encroach upon its province, and the understanding upon its part is equally active in mistake.

Thus we find man at his best estate provided for the affairs of life and of religion. The man whose feelings are healthily trained and given full play is perhaps best off; yet he never fails, both in life and in religion, to take up notions and to adopt practices which his neighbour's cold understanding can prove unreasonable. But your able man, who requires a proof for everything and takes nothing for granted upon the bidding of his heart, misses some of the very best things in life, and if religion is to be like life it would be very surprising that the able man should be the one to be always right in that sphere. Contemplating the relations so constantly and, as it might appear, necessarily inharmonious, of the active powers and the understanding, some have been led to pessimism: that is to say, to the belief of a source of inevitable mistake and unhappiness in the constitution of life, flowing more and more freely as the higher developments of life are reached. And in truth there would be little possibility of avoiding such a conclusion if we did not believe in the possibility of attaining a better balance of intellect and feeling, and in a steady progress of mental evolution towards good ends: a general progress which will not be prevented by the doubts or difficulties of this person or of that. It is impossible to believe in such a progress without believing in a Power which directs it, and that belief is in itself religion. Moreover, the progress itself has included faith in the supernatural.

7. *Securus judicat orbis terrarum.* This is a phrase which ought by right to have a far more true and literal meaning for believers in evolution of every degree than it had for the thinker who first propounded it. St. Augustine

[sidenote: Evolution must take account of the inheritance of religion handed down in the human race.]

had in his mind the general agreement of the Christian world in opposition to private or sectarian opinions. But the *orbis terrarum* which the evolutionist deals with is not only the whole human race but the whole universe whose progress from time immemorial finds its crowning result in the present condition of the mind of man. Nevertheless, there are no sort of people who are more confident than evolutionists that a trim argument is capable of wiping out from the nature of a man or of a race the religious thoughts and feelings which have been confirmed by the experience of ages. And this, though the very faculties of reason by which this destructive feat is performed have to the evolutionist no other sanction or foundation than that actual existence in the present development of man, of which in the case of religion he makes so little account. This point has been ably pressed from the negative side by Mr. Arthur Balfour:—

"Ever since there has been speculation in the varieties of religious opinion this fact must have been obvious, that a man's beliefs are very much the results of antecedents and surroundings with which they have no logical connection. . . . In other words, it must have been always known that there were causes of belief which were not reasons. ... But though in the face of such evidence nobody doubts the fact, few people, I should think, contemplate it habitually without suffering under a sort of sceptical uneasiness when they consider its bearings on their own opinions. ... The existence of Comtism is explained by it no less than that of fetichism; it accounts for theories of evolution not less than for Hindoo cosmogonies, and the man of science is as certainly under its control as was the Indian whose superstitions he is making the subject of analysis and classification."[1]

But to be sure there is a positive side to the same principle. We are what we are. We cannot help using the faculties and working upon the principles which have been developed in us, according to the laws laid down for us by the facts of our state. If we do this truly we know that future development through it may indefinitely enlarge the faculties and surround them with different facts, yet never will prove it otherwise than right that, being what we are and where we

[1] *Defence of Philosophic Doubt*, pp. 360-2.

are, we should think according to our condition. The question is, what are our faculties and what is our condition? And this is not a question which a man can decide for himself off-hand by giving unrestrained scope to the faculty, be it sentiment or understanding, which pushes forward most vehemently in his existing state of mind. Many, perhaps most, men discover, even in the after portion of their own lives, how they may misconceive themselves. They must call the experiences and powers of their race to supplement their own. Even these must be tested so far as a man can do it. For that may pretend to be history which is not real history, and those may pretend to be assured and developed powers of man which are only exercises of his imagination. It is here that analogy is of great use.

The question whether we are called upon to do any act, either mental or physical, is ruled by the question whether we have the power to do it, including in the word power both the faculty in us and the state of outward circumstances which affords the faculty opportunity to work. If we have the power, then its very possession is generally sufficient reason why we should attempt to use it; and inducements of various kinds may be added to an indefinite extent by the example or influence of other men and by the good which the act may promise to ourselves. But if we have not the power no amount of inducement should prevail to make us waste our energies on an impossible task. When we are considering such a matter the most effective resolution of the question whether we have the power will be found in an instance where we ourselves, or somebody else whose faculties are like our own, have performed a task which offered similar difficulties. Suppose that we felt a call to learn a foreign language, either from a desire to exercise our linguistic faculty, or to obtain knowledge of the thoughts of some who have spoken or written in that language alone. If there be absolutely no means whatever of learning the language we must give up the attempt, however much it costs us to do so. But if it can be shown us that other people, or we ourselves, have learnt another language which presented the same difficulties our course will be clear, and nothing will prevent an immediate attempt to master this foreign tongue except our failure to apprehend the good which we can derive from knowing it; a failure of which aversion to labour and the desire to spend our time more pleasantly will be the most probable account. Religion is this foreign language, and Bishop Butler would persuade us that whatever difficulties it may offer we have got over similar ones in accepting the laws of life.

8. But Bishop Butler makes an assumption which is so far from being considered allowable in the present state of thought that it gives opportunity to some of saying that the usefulness of his work has passed away. A great error no doubt; but still it is obvious that the needs of those who doubt the existence of a personal God cannot be wholly met by a book which assumes that fact. The brief hint which Butler gives of the methods by which he considers the existence of a personal God to be proved, includes that of analogy, but he gives no details. To underpin his work with a proof of the being of God by means of the same great principle on which the rest of the structure depends, must be the office of some mind as great as his. But the matter is of such importance that to give a few humble hints

Subject of the following pages: an attempt to show the analogy between our knowledge of man and our knowledge of God.

towards its solution, or even to start the question, may be better than to have remained silent on it. The object, then, of the following pages will be to show, firstly, that there is such an analogy between belief in personal man and in a personal God, that whoever accepts the one is thereby proved capable of attaining to the other ; and, secondly, that not only do the same difficulties meet us in believing human personality as those we have to face in believing that of God, but the perplexities in our knowledge of human nature are inexplicable unless we follow that knowledge out into that divine sphere to which its analogies lead us.

That we have a certain knowledge, not merely of the personality of this or that man, but of human personality in general, is certain. It commences in feelings and experiences long prior to our capacity for formulating any theory on the subject; and many people never formulate any theory upon it at all. But the course of one's inward thoughts or one's controversy with others may make it so necessary to state for ourselves the theory of man's nature that our practical treatment of humanity in ourselves or in others may suffer total change for the worse if we neglect the task.

When it is necessary to give a name to that essential notion of human nature, in which we sum up our knowledge of it, we all think of this word Personality. Sometimes, indeed, we apply the word superficially enough; as when we call any additional knowledge we acquire of a man's appearance, manners, or even dress, an addition to our knowledge of his personality. If these externals, however, were all the word implies there would be no reason why we should apply it to man alone and deny it to dogs and horses, which have also their peculiarities of manner and appearance. But without pretending to decide the question how far that which makes man's personality is or is not a higher degree of that which is found in the lower animals, it is still a fact that we restrict the word to man. Manners and appearance form parts of personality only by reason of their connection with a deeper quality either peculiar to man, or if it be common to other animals, yet not known or felt by us to be so. We shall not, however, spend time in discussing the word personality. We but use it as summing up, as well as any word can do, our peculiar knowledge of man. If we be led to any theory of human nature which denies our peculiar knowledge of man, an immense alteration will be worked in our practical relations to other men. We are about, therefore, to inquire what it is that is implied in human personality thus understood, and under what conditions we hold the knowledge; intending then to ask the further question whether we do not know God in the same way. And for the reasons before stated we shall conduct the inquiry with reference not merely to man's intellectual convictions, but his practical feelings.

9. We shall suppose that a man goes out for a walk upon some fine summer's day. All nature around him, from the sun in the heavens above him to the grass, the leaves, and the water, is in correspondence with his senses, and through them with his mind. *In spite of the sympathies we have with nature we restrict personality to man.* He can individualise each of the innumerable organisations which make up nature, as a tree, a flower, a bird, and so forth. With each of these he can put himself in correspondence by opening to it the particular faculties of his frame to which it is adapted, as sight or hearing, smell or taste. When this is done the object never fails to respond and make

itself felt. Were he so minded he could devote further attention to any one of these innumerable objects; and if he did so it would reveal more and more of itself, both to sense and mind, with various effects of pleasure and instruction. This more particular attention has been often called the questioning of nature; and the phrase scarcely implies a metaphor. For although the particular bodily faculties which we use in asking questions of nature are different from those we use in asking questions of men, yet the process is essentially the same. There is the same willingness in our minds to receive knowledge, and the same resort to our bodily faculties in order to seek the knowledge; be it the tongue, the touch, or the eye, there is no essential difference. There is the same responsive experience of sensations by which the desired knowledge is conveyed, be it through ear, or eye, or hand. And in each case the mind gathers up the sensations and carries them within to make what it can of them, be that less or more. So far there is no essential difference between the relation of other natural objects to our faculties of knowledge and that which is borne by man.

When we come to animal life the resemblance

to human intercourse is still closer. Your dog runs beside you. Like yourself and like other men he is an organism moving freely over the ground. His movements are governed by powers residing in his own frame to a degree not different from that physical self-guidance which you can claim for yourself and for the rest of mankind. He is capable not merely of being addressed by touch or sight, as is the case with inanimate things, but of hearing your words, understanding your looks, and shewing such sympathy with the feelings which you express even unconsciously to yourself, as some of your fellow-men cannot furnish. He will come at the sound of his name, will fetch when you bid him, will be depressed or joyful according to your mood; and, on the other hand, his cheerful bark and lively movements can communicate his mood to you almost as well as words convey those of man, and sometimes better. He is a happier being than man if it be indeed true that, while he has a superior being to love and trust, man has none.

In the course of your walk you meet another man. He may be a very unattractive figure indeed, and very probably you pass him by without exchanging a single word with him. If you do speak to him you may well discover that his power of understanding you is extremely restricted. You may find yourself much more at home with your dog. The larger number of your questions and observations may fall quite as dead upon his ear as if they had been addressed to some inanimate object. This comparison indeed readily occurs to us, and we say that one might as well have been talking to a stone as to such a man. Like the tree or like the dog the man presents himself as a mass of matter which is in correspondence and communication with your senses and with your mind to a certain limited extent. But when upon your return from your walk you are asked how many *persons* you met, you will say, only one. The beauty of the various things and creatures which you have seen and conversed with, and whose influence you have so deeply felt, the pleasure they have given you, the instruction they have communicated, will altogether fail in inducing you to confer upon any of them the title person.

This would be a small matter if it were not for the implications which this word carries with it

There would be nothing more strange in our applying the mere word person to an erect two-legged animal than in giving the word dog to one with four legs. But how much the word implies. Very probably you consider that it implies immortality in the being to whom you ascribe it. You consider a person as above the changes of matter to a degree which you do not ascribe to any other being. Even if you do not believe in the immortality of persons you will acknowledge that most of mankind have done so, and that there is a kind of appropriateness in the idea, and an anomaly in the death of persons which you do not feel in the extinction of things. Persons are in correspondence with yourself in a way which despite of all partial resemblances differs essentially from that which is held by non-personal organisms. You ascribe to persons a position in the scale of being altogether different from these, and, perhaps you will add, superior to them.

10. Even if a man be not of a very meditative turn of mind he may well pause and ask himself why it is that he puts such a difference between some of the appearances which pass across his vision and others. Such

Why do we make this difference?

a question may be due to the vague scepticism of feeling which comes over us and bids us doubt the warrant of any step in knowledge beyond our immediate sensations. But physical science is deliberate in its utterances, and speaks on good ground, and it, too, seems to bid us unify all outward things in themselves and in their relation to us. It traces the course of our own sensations and the impressions by which outward things gain access to us, and it gives a physical aspect to the whole process, whether the impression be that which makes us think of a person or that which makes us think of a thing. And when, passing from our means of attaining the knowledge of the outward world, it regards the world in itself, science shows us that the laws which govern the forces and the movements of nature extend also to man. It excepts no man, and nothing in man, from the persistent operation of these laws, and it tells us of nothing in man which is not their result. It professes in these latter days even to display to us the various steps of the process by which from the lowest stage of life, if not from a point lower still, the mind of the creatures is developed stage after stage until we arrive at the mind of man. And if this be really the whole and sufficient account of the matter, upon what does our right depend of calling man a person when we refuse the title to any other organism?

11. Is it upon the particular character of man's outward form as conveyed to us by the perceptions of our senses, or upon any peculiar beauty supposed to belong to it? That cannot be what constitutes a person; at least it cannot be that in which the distinctive quality which we attach to man resides, be that quality expressed by the word person or not. Many other forms appear to us quite as wonderful and quite as beautiful as that of man. It would be a strange account of the matter, and would not in the least meet the facts, to maintain that though we refuse the name of person to a tree standing erect with head and limbs, and to a dog moving freely over the ground, yet when we see a form at once erect and in free motion we give it the name of person, with all the wonderful implications included in the word. *We do not find personality in our perception of the material organisation of men.*

Does the distinctive idea of man reside then in the subtle and delicate character of the organism which we know to underlie his outward form, and in the curious and complicated action which results in his life? The fact is that under the form of a tree, and even under forms much lower still, there lie adjustments which are infinitely wonderful and infinitely beyond our understanding. The smallest leaf that grows affords us in its origin and the provision for its life overwhelming evidence of this. And though there may be in man a greater number and complexity of such arrangements, we cannot justly say that he is physically more wonderful than those other things which have been admitted to be infinitely wonderful; infinity is not capable of degrees. The same may be said of the results of the adjustments as of the adjustments themselves. We cannot understand at all better how the flower produces on us the impressions of colour and scent, than how the poet gives forth his verse for our delight. Wonderful as the latter result may be, it yet differs only in degree from the former. And any reasons for calling the poet a person, which are founded merely upon his curious organisation and the wondrous results which it sends out to the world, must inevitably give way when we consider without prejudice the claims of his humbler rivals.

12. It may be suggested that, apart from the connection between the intellect of man and his organisation, intellect itself is a possession of such a distinctive character as to stamp its owner with a peculiar character and demand a peculiar title, even if that title should prophesy for him a future destiny different from that of all the world besides. Now intellect is a word which in a loose way may be taken to designate the whole inward constitution of man. And if the expression be used thus widely we must needs conceive man's distinctive quality to lie in his intellect, because we have already decided that it cannot lie in his outward form. But most people will allow that it is only a loose and inaccurate application of the word intellect which lets into it so wide a signification. Nearly every one would reply to the question, whether man's inward constitution includes anything besides intellect, by admitting that it does. A man composed of body and intellect alone might be in some respects above, but would be in more important respects below, the normal and proper type of man.

Nor in the intelligence we perceive in them.

When we take the word intellect in its proper

signification of understanding and as denoting only a part of the inward powers and endowments of man, we must feel the greatest doubt whether the reason why we set man so entirely apart from other things and from other animals can be found in his intellect. How is it possible, for instance, to deny intellect to those of the lower animals whose lives are so closely united with that of man? The usefulness of dogs and of horses to us depends not upon their brute strength but upon their capacity for education, and their power of understanding our objects and contributing to them. The pleasure which we derive from their companionship consists in watching and in developing that which we cannot but call their intelligence. A hundred phrases in common use and a hundred daily experiences show how men believe in the intellect of these friends and instruments of their mental life. If we consider how we treat them and how they respond to our treatment, it will seem more difficult to say why it is that we refuse them the title of person than to point to the distinctive quality in man because of which we give it to him.

13. We must upon the whole pronounce it

impossible to say upon what grounds of purely outward experience, comparing man as an object of observation with the other objects with which we hold converse in life, we can set him so apart from them as we do. *It is found first in our own self-consciousness and then ascribed to other men.* The question then arises, what can we find in man beyond our outward experience of him and his manifestations of himself, in which his personality can consist, and how other men attain to the knowledge of it? Now St. Paul, in a well-known passage, instructs us that knowledge of the secrets of human nature springs up first within a man's own breast, and thence is communicated to others. "What man knoweth the things of a man, save the spirit of man which is in him?" (1 Cor. ii. 11.) And this is the account of our distinctive feeling about other men which probably most of us will accept. Our knowledge that other men possess personality depends upon our knowledge that we have it ourselves. Nothing could possibly have revealed to us the thought of such a thing if we had not found the consciousness of it within. We seem driven to adopt this account of our belief in the personality of other men by sheer inability to

discover any other method of accounting for it. The idea which the word expresses is excessively marked and distinctive, and our feeling towards those to whom we apply it is as different as possible from that which we have to other beings and things; yet it is impossible to discover the ground for this in the difference between human beings as objects of our observation, and the other myriad objects which meet us in the world. But we can account for the matter on the principle that other persons are to us not merely objects, but such objects as are a kind of repetition or image of our own subjective consciousness.

We are thrown back, therefore, upon our knowledge of our own personality. And in order to make our analysis in anywise complete, we must proceed to consider how and on what conditions it is that we possess any such knowledge of ourselves. We shall then have to inquire what grounds we have for extending the same belief to other people. Now, to ask what we mean by our personality is to ask what we mean by the words "I myself."

14. When we ask that question we are speedily struck by the fact that we do not use the phrase

"I myself" with uniformity, but sometimes include in its signification a great many things which at other times we exclude from it.

Thus a general might say, "I myself fell upon the enemy's army"—appearing to include within his own self the whole mass of men which moves at his command. A man might say, "I myself, while living in England was calumniated in India," thus comprising within the self of a man living in England a kind of atmosphere of reputation extending to the most distant parts of the world. Doubtless, it will be said that these are metaphorical and figurative ways of speech. This need not be questioned. But it will be very hard to show that they are more figurative or improper than many other ways of speech which pass for being perfectly literal. Suppose one to say "I struck him," the word "I" might well be thought to be here used in an entirely literal sense. If so, the self which the word "I" denotes must include the hand with which the blow was struck. But when we use the equivalent expression "I struck him with my hand," we see at once that the hand is regarded not as a part of the self but as a possession of the self

The extension of the phrase "I myself," is not always the same.

which it uses as its instrument. The very words "my hand" show that the hand is not a part of the self, but something of which the self regards itself as owner to use as it may desire. If this were a mere matter of words it would not be worth mentioning. But it corresponds to our consciousness and to the facts of the case. When we say "I struck him" we really do mean to include the hand in the self, and yet, when we say "my hand" we really feel and really mean to say that the hand is objective to the self, and stands outside of it and is possessed by it, not otherwise than the house in which the man lives.

We go further inward and ask whether, if the hand with which the blow was struck is not a part of the self, the notion or the passion which has originated the blow is not a part of it. But it is not. We say my notions and my passions. And when we use these phrases we really imply that our central self is felt to be something different from the notions or passions which belong to it or characterise it for a time. The reality of the self subsists underneath these colours of its life and subsists when they are gone, just as a wall might pass under various species of decoration yet never receive any of them below its surface. Beliefs and feelings are things which belong to, but are not, the genuine self. Thus our central self retires before our thought like some retreating army which takes up one position after another: as each is carried it is found that the self is not there but further within. Each power, each acquirement, each habit appears successively first as a part of the man as others know him and as he thinks of himself, and then as something which the self can hold from it and declare to be separate.[1]

15. And how far might this process go on? Could we ever reach some capacity or some quality so central that we should be able to say, not in any mere colloquial sense but in all senses, "This is myself. From this I cannot imagine myself to be separated or distinguished; I cannot imagine myself calling this *mine* but always *me*"? We never could

In the last resort the meaning of the phrase "I myself" runs up into a mystery.

---

[1] "It may appear not a paradox merely but a contradiction to say that the organism is at once within and without the mind, is at once subjective and objective, is at once *ego* and *non ego*, but so it is."—Sir W. Hamilton. [*Reid's Works*, p. 880, note.] It is plain that the very same double treatment which Hamilton here applies to the body is applicable to the mind. Mind, as well as body, denotes something that may be objective and may be subjective.

find any such quality. Whatever faculty either of body or of mind can be grasped and represented to the mind turns out also to be something which the central self puts from it, and with which it refuses to be identified. And thus when our mental faculties strive to grasp our own nature they are always baulked. They find ever before them a mystery. They have the power to recognize the existence of the self, and it never vanishes from them into nothingness; but they have no power to understand its nature or to tell what it is. It is real, the most certain reality in all life; the very pivot on which life turns; that in comparison of which not only our material possessions, our state and circumstances, not only our body and all its parts and powers without and within, but even our mind, with all its habits and endowments, must be pronounced external and unessential.[1] And yet this

---

[1] Peters, *Willenswelt und Weltwille*, pp. 293, 294.

"Show a man to himself as a material thing; take out of his brain his pineal gland, or whatever else you please, and presenting it to him on a plate say, '*That*, sir, is you, your *ego*': the exhibition, supposing it possible, would instantly prove that the self so shown was not himself, for the man would say, ' I know myself along with that material thing.' "—Ferrier's *Institutes of Metaphysic*, p. 221.

" I am not the anger or the pain which I experience, any more than I am the chair or the table which I perceive."—*Ibid.* p. 232.

essential self cannot be made the subject of thought: it is known not in itself but in its effects.[1]

We may rest assured that the sense of this mysterious reality at the centre of our own being is not a mere puzzle for the weak and ignorant. Some of the strongest thinkers have recognized it.[2] And though there are schools which in their repugnance to mysteries have refused to acknowledge anything in the self except a bundle of sensations and thoughts, or capacities of sensations

---

[1] "It is not by any after-effort of reflection that I combine together sight and hearing, thought and volition, into a factitious unity or compounded whole: in each case I am immediately conscious of myself seeing and hearing, willing and thinking. This self-personality like all other simple and immediate presentations is indefinable: but it is so, because it is superior to definition. The extravagant speculations in which metaphysicians attempted to explain the nature and properties of the soul as it is not given in consciousness, furnish no valid ground for renouncing all inquiry into its character as it is given as *a power conscious of itself*."—Mansel's *Prolegomena Logica*, p. 139.

[2] *Willenswelt und Weltwille*, pp. 84, 99, 99, and the passages gathered from Kant.

"The thoughts and feelings of which we are conscious are continually changing: but something which I call myself remains under this change of thought. This self has the same relation to all the successive thoughts I am conscious of—they are all my thoughts. If any man asks a proof of this, I confess I can give none; there is an evidence in the proposition itself which I am unable to resist. Shall I think that thought can stand by itself without a thinking being? or that ideas can feel pleasure or pain?" —*Reid's Works by Hamilton*, p. 443.

and thought, yet the impossibility of ignoring the something which is felt as existing behind every feeling has proved too strong for their systems, and again and again they have been found admitting the mysterious reality, and acknowledging that nothing which can be told to man of the structure of his body, nor yet of the faculties of his mind, can reveal to him what he is in himself.[1]

[1] Mr. J. S. Mill's conception of the *ego* (*Examination of Sir W. Hamilton*, chapter xii.) does not essentially differ from that of Hume. "If we speak of the mind as a series of feelings we are obliged to complete the statement by calling it a series of feelings which is aware of itself as past and future: and we are reduced to the alternative of believing that the mind or *ego* is something different from any series of feelings or possibilities of them or of accepting the paradox that something which *ex hypothesi* is but a series of feelings, can be aware of itself as a series. The truth is that we are here face to face with that final inexplicability at which, as Sir W. Hamilton observes, we inevitably arrive when we reach ultimate facts." Thus we have Mr. Mill admitting that there is a mystery in the *ego* however you take it. We have, he says, but to choose between two statements of the nature of the mystery; either, (1), that the *ego* is something different from the series of feelings and possibilities of them, or (2), that it is not only a series of feelings and possibilities of them, but has the strange and paradoxical quality that it is also a sense of the possibility of a series of feelings past and future. Mr. Mill prefers the latter statement of the case, but we unhesitatingly pronounce for the other. First, because when he offers the word "mind" as the complete equivalent of *ego*, he thereby shows that he does not realise the problem which the words "I myself" present, and which consists in this, that we feel ourselves to be something so far different from our minds as well as from our bodies that the one as much as the

And yet the structure of his body and the analysis of his mind convey to man the revelation of things which deeply concern his true self although they do not constitute it, and which show him the work of his self and the means by which his self may be dealt with even while it remains in its essence a mystery to him. To tell the nature of the instruments with which I must work and without the use of which I cannot make even my existence known, is to tell me something of myself; to relate what I have done in time gone by by means of these instruments, is to tell me the history of myself and of my

other must be regarded as a possession of the self, and therefore not identical with it. Second, because the abstract term "possibility of feeling" is quite inadequate to express the concrete notion we have of ourselves as beings who are capable of feeling; and leaves wholly out of account the knowledge which accompanies every present feeling, that it is felt by some one and implies the existence of something besides itself. The same observations apply to Professor Huxley's defence of Hume's position (*English Men of Letters*, Hume, chapter ix.). When Hume says "I never can catch myself without a perception, and never can observe anything but the perception," we may quite agree with the first clause, for it actually implies the recognition of two things, "myself" and "a perception." But this not only does not imply, but actually contradicts, the second clause, in which Hume plainly intimates that he can catch the perception without the self; which is, perhaps, the hardiest statement, says Professor Ferrier, ever hazarded in philosophy.

E

doings in the past. And the same history tells how self may be reached and affected, namely, through those faculties which are known to be in constant contact with it.

II.

SELF-KNOWLEDGE.

"What man knoweth the things of a man, save the spirit of man which is in him?"—1 COR. ii. 11.

16. WE use the words "I" and "myself" with various extensions of meaning. But these various uses fall into two great classes which we may call the historical or objective, and the active or subjective meanings of the term. *[Two aspects in which we are presented to ourselves. 1. Historically: as filling a place in the world,]*

By the historical meaning of the phrase "I myself" is denoted that use of the words by which we set ourselves apart from ourselves, and contemplate the body and the mind which belong to us as filling a place in the world, and having a past history which may be remembered and a future history which may be foreseen. When we remember the sayings and doings of this "I myself" as they have proceeded and are still proceeding, they, and the organism which has enacted them, fill a place as objective to our thought as any other organism in the world. This *ego* is part of the system of things; its action is determined by what surrounds it, and by the forces which it includes within itself. Very often our meaning would be nearly as well conveyed by substituting our name for the words "I myself" in recalling to ourselves what we remember of the part which the organism we call ours has performed in the world. And this, as certain metaphysicians have remarked, is what children and childish people are prone to do. They say, "Baby did it," or the like, instead of "I did it."

To be sure this does not express the whole past fact as it is felt by people whose minds are developed, and even probably in some vague way by these childish minds themselves. The objective form of the action takes possession of their minds; but probably not so entirely that the subjective absolutely vanishes. Can we believe that when the child says "Baby did it," there is absolutely no difference to it except in the vividness of the impression which the action has made on its own mind between this act and one which it has seen done by some one else? It is probably true that though the outward, and, so to speak, impersonal form of the act be the most prominent to the child, there is hidden underneath it a germ of that self-consciousness which in after years will make the objective and impersonal aspect of all present or vividly realised actions secondary, and the personal form expressed by the word "I" the primary and prominent form under which he thinks of them.[1] It is certain that the latter is the way in which we think of our actual doings when our minds have come to maturity. Along with all the historical and objective representation which sets "myself" before the mind as simply part of the world's scene, and as an operation of the forces and powers of nature, there abides also a kind of consciousness of a deeper and more personal connection of an inner self with the business.[2]

---

[1] But see Jeanmaire, *L'Idée de la Personnalité* (Paris, 1882), p. 180.

[2] "It is the empirical consciousness which informs me that there are in myself perceptions, remembrances, representations, and internal diversity: it is the transcendental consciousness which furnishes me with the idea represented by the word 'I,' the subject always the same and identical."—Kant. See Jeanmaire, pp. 93-103, and his criticisms, pp. 116, 119.

17. Upon this consciousness apparently depends our sense of personal identity. Very great stress has been laid upon the wonderful continuity which this sense establishes in our lives, whereby we are assured that among surroundings the most various, and under changes of bodily form and of mental acquirement and disposition, we are still the same individuals. And this is certainly a remarkable class of facts. But we must not forget the important part which the objective representation of self holds in our remembrance of past actions, especially when they become distant and are thought of more as events than as actions. We are even capable of supposing that we ourselves took part in scenes which we have frequently imagined—as King George IV. believed that he had been present at Waterloo. And in dreams there seems to be a kind of successive transfer of the sense of self from one party in a scene to another, so that it is hard to say whether each person who speaks or acts becomes to us for the moment the "I myself" or whether there is properly no "I myself" present to consciousness at all.

<small>and as having a sense of personal identity.</small>

18. It seems that it is in the very moment of

conscious action that the presence and power of the mysterious *ego* is really felt.¹ As action proceeds this mysterious self comes in every successive moment out of its obscurity into life and work. Not one unit of time, even the most minute which imagination can reach, elapses before the mysterious self puts on the familiar forms of human life and action. No mind can ever see it uninvested with these or imagine what it is without them.² The clothing of life covers the whole figure of the self. We feel that it does not constitute the true self; but this true self cannot be represented in thought or described. For representation in thought the inward self is caught up into the self of observation; in which aspect its desires, its thinking, its mental life appear to follow lines as invariable and as physically caused as the rails which compel

<small>2. Actively as mysterious agents setting the forces of the world in operation.</small>

---

[1] Jeanmaire, p. 196. "The continuity of my individual existence ought not to be confounded with the direct intuition of my identity."

[2] "The *ego never* can be known as a completed non-material existence, because it can be known only as the universal element of all cognition; but this universal element by itself—that is, dissociated from any particular element—is absolutely unknowable; and therefore if the reader expects a proof of the existence of himself as a completed immaterial entity, irrespective of his association with all particular things and all determinate states, he must for ever be disappointed."—Ferrier, *Institutes of Metaphysics*, p. 248.

a locomotive engine to hold its course. The power of physical surroundings in mental history is undeniable; the same external causes and the same internal motives must invariably produce the same actions. Vain is the imagination that we can strive against our circumstances and against the motives which operate most strongly upon our bodily and mental frame. And thus we think of ourselves in the past, and all the way up to the very verge of the moment of our actual existence; and thus we regard ourselves in the future all the way forward from that moment. As the notion of a tree is made up of the place where it is planted, and of the appearance which it presents, and of the functions of growth and movement with which we know it to be endowed and from which certain results may invariably be anticipated, so also it is with man. He presents himself to his own thought with only such difference from the tree as is caused by the greater complexity of the functions which a man performs. So much is this the case that the question has been raised whether after all, this is not the only sense in which the word "I" can be used; and whether our perception of the place which our body and our mind take in the series of the world's history is not all that we mean by our self and all that constitutes our self-consciousness.

But if this were so, all that really gives us the sense of either possession or responsibility in the sayings and doings of the self would vanish. We should find ourselves looking idly upon the movements of our mind and our moral nature precisely as we look upon the involuntary twitching of muscles in our feet, or feel the beating of our heart, or notice in the glass that our hair is getting grey. Nay, it would seem that we must needs take still a further step, and break the slender bond by which even such purely physical changes belong to ourselves and are said to happen to us. Everything in us would pass imperceptibly into the system of nature without any real distinction between the two. Not only would there be no "myself" but nothing would be mine at all. And this will always be found a practical absurdity which we cannot bring ourselves to face.[1]

19. There is an argument arising from the very nature of thought which has been considered to prove that the

Self cannot be directly known as a subject;

[1] Jeanmaire, p. 200.

historical or objective sense of the *ego* is the only one that can be known to us. Nothing (it is urged) can be known to us except as an object of thought. Therefore even we ourselves, when we become objects of our own thought, lose our subjective character. The object is unthinkable. Even in such elementary actions of the self as are expressed by the words "I think," the "I" when we try to grasp it must become an object; and if it does it falls into the same category as the rest of the things we bring before our minds. The "I" which thinks will be something just as much known and just as little known as the rest of the things in the world. There will be no difference. Everything has in it an unknowable element, and runs up in its origin and in its existence to something which cannot be understood. So and no otherwise, will it be with the self. It will be like everything else, a wonderful and incomprehensible item in a wonderful and incomprehensible system of things. The very nature of thought forbids it to be conceived in any other way.

It has sometimes been replied to this reasoning that somehow or other the subject can be thought of as subject.[1] But that does not appear to be possible;[2] we cannot think of ourselves without placing ourselves as objects before our own minds, and therefore regarding ourselves as being or doing some one of those thinkable facts which can alone make us capable of being represented. We must stir the surface of the world's affairs somehow before it can be known even to ourselves that we are there at all. But a better reply is that though the subject cannot, as such, be made matter of thought, yet thought seems quite capable of grasping the fact that the subject exists. For instance, when we say "I think," we predicate the act of thinking which we can understand, of a subject "I," which on trial we find we cannot understand at all. To understand it we have to make an object of it and call it a thinking power, but our understanding is quite equal to seeing that the "I" is something different from the act of thinking, and that this appears from the very

[1] See Professor Momerie, *Agnosticism*, p. 37. I cannot agree with the argument of the same clever writer: "If we know ourselves, all knowledge does not imply the relation of subject and object."—*Personality*, p. 40.

[2] "As regards internal intuition we cognise our own subject only as phenomenon, and not as it is in itself."—Kant, *Critique of Pure Reason*, Meiklejohn's translation, p. 95. (See Professor Caird, *Philosophy of Kant*, pp. 334, 401.)

words "I think" themselves. For if the "I" were not something separable from the thinking, and had not an existence apart from it, then "I think" would be merely equivalent to the proposition "that which thinks, thinks," and this does not represent the felt reality of the case.[1] Thus the very argument advanced to prove the empirical nature of the *ego* is that which shows us most clearly that we are in presence of a mystery in ourselves—an inward and personal mystery clearly distinguishable from the general mystery which encompasses all things. For if nothing can be known to us save as an object, then the subject of knowledge must be something we cannot know; yet the very assertion that we know implies the existence of such a subject. And this is, and ever must remain, a mystery.

Mr. Herbert Spencer maintains that it is an

---

[1] "Man is a phenomenon of the sensuous world, and at the same time, therefore, a natural cause, the causalty of which must be regulated by natural laws. As such, he must possess an empirical character like all other natural phenomena. . . . But man, to whom nature reveals itself only through sense, cognises himself not only by his senses, but also through pure apperception. . . . He is thus to himself, on the one hand, a phenomenon, but, on the other hand, in respect of certain faculties, a purely intelligible object—intelligible because its action cannot be ascribed to sensuous receptivity."—Kant, *Critique of Pure Reason*, ed. Bohn, p. 338.

illusion to suppose that the self at each moment is anything more than the aggregate of feelings and ideas, actual and nascent, which then exists.[1] Is he right in this? When we say "*my feelings*" we imply, according to all the usage of language, the existence of feelings and of an owner of them. According to Mr. Spencer the feelings are real, but the owner of them is an illusion. But this is certainly not the case. Illusion is a word which has a definite meaning in the world of objects, and denotes a certain class of appearances among those with which life brings us in contact. When you have seen an illusion you have in the first place seen an appearance, and in the second place you have found out that appearance to be deceptive,

---

[1] *Elements of Psychology*, vol. i. p. 500. Professor Momerie (*Personality*, p. 47) remarks with justice that Mr. Herbert Spencer, in his *Psychology*, adopts the ordinary positive notion that the *ego* is nothing but the transitory state of the moment; but in his *First Principles*, though he denies that a permanent subject can be *known*, he distinctly asserts that it *exists*. Hence the hesitations and contradictions in Mr. Spencer, upon which M. Jeanmaire (*L'Idée de la Personnalité*, p. 34) remarks. It is exceedingly noteworthy, in reference to the argument of these lectures, that a precisely similar inconsistency is displayed by Mr. Spencer on the subject of religion to that which these writers note in reference to human personality. In the *First Principles*, religion appears as the persistent consciousness of a Power underlying what is seen; but in the *Sociology* religion is persistently ascribed to positive and experienced facts, either real or imaginary, as tribal chieftaincy, ghosts and the like.

and another appearance has been imaged and has permanently displaced the first in your mind. Now, is this the case with that "something more" than the aggregate of feelings and ideas which we suppose to exist, and which Mr. Spencer pronounces to be illusion? On the contrary, it obstinately remains with all its mystery, and refuses to allow any idea, however clear, to displace it. Indeed even upon the ground of clearness Mr. Spencer's theory has little to boast. When I feel, what, according to him, is that which feels? Is it the actual present or nascent feeling itself? That is contrary to the very form of the expression "I feel," and turns it into a meaningless proposition. Is it the other feelings of which the man is capable, but which are not then present? That cannot be, because they are not present. The supposed illusion will not give way, and every one would confess that to substitute for the words "I feel" the words "the aggregate of my feelings and ideas, actual and nascent, feels" would be quite out of the question. Even for the sake of making things clear we are obliged to believe in a mystery within ourselves.

20. But we can well understand why Mr.

Spencer makes this contention. It is because no other sense of the word "I" than that of an aggregate of thoughts and feelings is known to physical science or to the faculty of understanding by which science works.[1] *and the objective sense of ourself is the only one known to science.* Only on condition of coming into the sequence of physical causation can the self be subjected to scientific thought. And if scientific thought be our only and sufficient source of knowledge, the mysterious sense of the word "self" must be got rid of. Yet it maintains its ground, and requires acknowledgment as a prior condition of that conscious life which we must have in order to know anything. Science has no right to enter upon any of its possessions without first paying this homage to mystery, and making confession that although it claims to extend its domain over all nature, yet the self which can say "I know" is beyond nature and therefore beyond science. Accordingly, if the knowledge of physiology were ever so to extend as that we should know that the most elementary act of thinking is represented by and inseparably connected with a physical change

---

[1] See Leighton's definition of the understanding: "The faculty judging according to sense."—Coleridge's *Aids to Reflection*, vol. i. p. 163 (1843).

in the brain, and this change were proved to have as necessary a connection with other physical circumstances preceding as the rolling of a billiard ball has with the stroke of the cue; if all human life inward and outward were proved to be natural and contained in nature, and all nature were shown to be inevitably bound together in a chain of physical causation—all this would never go any way towards proving that this mysterious "I myself" did not exist outside the system. It would be a mystery certainly, though not a greater mystery then than it is in the present condition of our knowledge. But though a mystery it would be a fact, the recognition of which we could no more avoid than we can leap off our own shadow.

21. If it be acknowledged that there is a mysterious or unembodied sense, as well as a palpable or embodied sense of our self, a question of very great importance is presented to us. Which of these two senses is that which is in daily use for the commerce of life? It is true indeed that the two senses of the word are actually mingled together, so that the embodied sense

<small>But the mysterious subjective self is that which we have in daily use.</small>

is never used so purely as not to have something of the mysterious in it, and the mysterious can never come into life or thought without the embodied. But which side of the *ego*, the known or the unknown, is that which we practically present to ourselves and to other people as life proceeds? It might be, that while a mystery had to be acknowledged in the matter this mystery should lie so far away from human life that we should never need to think of it. Everything, as Mr. Spencer so well shows us, runs up into mystery if you examine it closely enough; the very notion of a steam-engine runs up into mystery in several directions. But the steam-engine is practically quite well known to us. We know how to work it, and could not know this better were there no mystery behind it at all. And so of all the rest of nature. It has a known side, and our business is to make it turn this known side towards us. And if this work were complete our practical relation to nature would be complete. The consideration of the mysterious side of nature is only for the poet, and multitudes of men live their lives through without ever thinking of it.

But we have to answer our question by

acknowledging that whatever be the case in nature it is *not* merely in this fashion that the unknowable and mysterious within our own personality presents itself. It is the known and palpable that is outside of our practical selves. The true active self, which in every feeling is the subject, that is to say, the power to feel, and in every act is the power to work—this is the mysterious self. It is the one indivisible "I myself" which abides through all changes, and not the composite self made up of an infinite number of organs, which is the self of the commerce of life. Of this we speak when we say "I think" and "I will." For though it be necessary, as we admit it to be, that in the very act of coming out into life, even so far as to say "I think," the unknowable self must entangle itself with the powers of the world and with physical forces—still *it* appears as the personage, and *they* are but its clothing.

When the thought, the feeling, and the action are past and have become matter of history, then the self which moved in them is congealed into a hard form which the intellect quite grasps ; the glow of action is past. But when we speak of the immediate act as it passes out from us, and before it has gathered round itself the clothing of history, then our words struggle to express—but cannot fully express it because it passes human words—an incomprehensible subject doing or feeling certain things which in themselves are comprehensible. This is the sense of the self with which we really could not dispense. A man's name might serve him nearly as well as the word "I" for relating his history past or to come. But in that present which is the really important time, because its moments as they pass make up life in its living character, the sense of the word "I," which implies a great mystery, cannot be put out of use. Can men, then, be agnostics as to their own being? In one sense they *must* be agnostics, for they cannot understand themselves. But if the word agnostic implies putting away from us that which we cannot understand as something which is unpractical and of which we need not think, then no man can be agnostic as to this mystery of his own existence. He may try to be so. He may turn away his eyes from the mystery and think only of what he understands about himself, but in every moment of life the incomprehensible nature of that self which performs the immediate practical work of living bears witness against him.

22. Now there is another word in constant use of which a similar account must be given to that which has been rendered of the phrase "I myself"; namely, the word "will." This word is found, after a very cursory examination, to be used with very various extensions. Sometimes it assumes a concrete form and denotes something perfectly comprehensible to the mind, filling a place in the material system of the world, and having a history in the sequence of events—as when we call a man's testamentary disposition his will. No doubt the actual document is called the will only in a figurative sense; though here we must remark that it is doubtful whether, when a man calls a piece of inscribed parchment his will, he is speaking more figuratively than when he calls his body himself. However, when we ask whether even the dispositions embodied in the document can be called in a strict sense the will of the man, we at once perceive that they cannot. The action of his will in the matter has not been complete or free In a large number of cases the

The will; various extensions of the word.

act of making a will at all is that very act which would have been most carefully avoided if his will had been free, for it gives away to some one else possessions which had been cherished and loved. But, besides this, the action of will in making a will has been limited by very close conditions; by the amount of the testator's property, which is very probably less by many degrees than he would wish it to be; by the nature of those objects of bounty which he knows or has within his reach—possibly objects very different from those he would have willed had willing been of any use. Therefore we find that what is called a man's will is an extremely composite result, having in it a certain infusion of an element proceeding from the man himself, but also an element of still more striking proportions, sternly fixed for him and refusing to yield to any exertion of his will.

This unyielding element proceeds from the laws of the world, and from the facts of the case. Let us set it aside and take the will as it proceeds from the man himself in that sense of self which includes his whole physical organism. Have we here pure will? Does that product of his habits, passions, and desires, which the man himself would declare to be his own genuine and unconstrained will, really deserve that title? Calm onlookers, and even he himself in calm reflection, can very well perceive that it is not so. The laws of his physical life, his bodily condition, the operation of motives suggested by inevitable outward circumstances which he did not create or cause—all these things limit his will and turn it into particular directions and give it a character. And very often people perceive that the character which circumstances unwilled by them have imposed upon their will is one which had much better not have been given, and which they had rather change but cannot. Seeing how invariable and unbending are the circumstances of life, and how entirely they envelope both our bodies and our minds, a great many very able writers have concluded that they cover the whole; in which case what we call will is nothing but the working of the human machine. Spinoza[1] is of opinion that the stone as it falls would, if it were conscious, think itself free, and with as much justice as man; for it

---

[1] Ep. 62. See Pollock's *Spinoza*, p. 208. Schopenhauer, *Die Welt als Wille und als Vorstellung*, vol. i. p. 150.

is doing that to which its constitution leads it, and no more can be said for him.

23. It is impossible to refute this as matter of theory. The physical circle runs from the outer world through the nervous system to the brain and back to the outer world again; the corresponding metaphysical circle runs from the outer world through motives to the mind and back again to the outer world. And these circles are alike complete.[1] But it is the intellect which alone informs us of their completeness, and the intellect is not the whole man nor has it any right to pronounce itself the sole exponent of the facts of his constitution. It has no right to regard the man of whom it forms a part as a machine, nor even as a machine provided with a curious ineffective apparatus of self-consciousness attached to it. Man is not only a thinking but a living being, and whatever

Determinism not to be refuted as a theory;

---

[1] " Une raison décisive s'oppose à ce que nous nous représentions le vouloir d'une manière intelligible : c'est que le vouloir, en lui-même, est l'acte propre du sujet conscient en tant que sujet, de sorte que faire abstraction du sujet dans sa fonction subjective c'est supprimer ce que fait le fond et l'essence du vouloir. Or c'est ce que nous faisons lorsque nous essayons de nous le représenter. Nous cherchons alors à prendre pour objet de notre pensée ce qui ne peut quitter la situation de sujet sans cesser d'exister."—Jeanmaire p. 208.

is necessary for life must appear in any true account of him. Now the system of determinism, physical or metaphysical, however it may seem true for thought, is not true for life. No investigation of the human physiology, and no argument upon the operation of motives, has any tendency to make us feel destitute of will at the moments of action; and those are the moments which in their succession make up life. Neither the past nor the future form any part of real life. It is only the present that can be truly said to be living, nor can life be really studied by any one except the living person. Even he can do it but imperfectly, since the living moment, as he tries to grasp it, passes into the dead past.

24. When we think upon the necessity which lies on us we find ourselves incapable of ever seizing its relation to the acts of life.

but false in practice.

Writers speak of the distinction between internal and external necessity, but it will be found on reflection that the distinction is futile, and that any necessity we can represent in thought must be really external to the act of intelligent life; the constraint which comes from the make of the body and the disposition of the mind is as much outside of the living act and as incommensurable with it as the physical constraint which comes from quite external circumstances. There is something entirely meaningless in saying that an act of will is constrained, since the word constrained has relation to a system of thought in which will in its true sense has no dwelling at all. Acknowledge in the fullest way the power of circumstance over you. Acknowledge that physical law takes possession of large portions of your life which once you were used to ascribe to unfettered will. Motives operate, and your physical system acts and is acted upon. But you never can trace either of these powers so far as to see it catch the will. Study as well as you can the operation both of physical law and internal motive. Weigh reasons with the utmost carefulness, or remember how they worked upon you. Be careful to forget no motive, not even the motive which may be furnished by the wish to act without a motive. Trace by the help of skilful physiologists the whole physical history of human action, until it becomes to you all as plainly ordered as the course of events when the sexton, duly paid, pulls the rope of the bell and by regular consequence the sound passes out of the tower. Still you know that at the critical moment there came out from the centre of your being an act which you can as little fit as a link in the chain of causation, mental or physical, as you can attach time to the hands of your watch. There is something in the act of will which refuses to be so bound. And this wonderful power is an intimate inalienable part of human consciousness which experiences its action without knowing what it is. It is one of the factors if not the chief factor of our life, which would not be our life without will: and it has a right to be recognised just as much as those other facts of consciousness on which our belief in causation depends.

25. Perhaps it will be said that the mystery of will is only the common mystery of all animate existence, and that the office of will is but to turn on the stream, while our physical circumstances and our tendencies of character determine the course that it is to run; just as the banks of the mill-race determine the course

We cannot separate intelligent choice from our conception of will.

of the water. But this is not our experience. We cannot divest our will of some share in determining the channel in which our energies are to run and the course they are to take.[1] We make bungling attempts at expressing the nature of this action of the will, and find no better way of doing so than by adopting the vocabulary of the external and material system; and we call it free. But we need not involve ourselves in the interminable controversy which that word suggests. Suffice it to say that if we must try to frame a complete and consistent system of human nature it will be necessary to include in it the free will of man; for there is that in the will which the intellect is incapable of expressing by any word but freedom. It is not subject to external constraint, and no constraint of any kind can be conceived which is not external to the will. If not to be subject to constraint is to be free, the will is free and carries its essential freedom with it, however small be its powers of making itself felt in the outer world. But

---

[1] "Jedes Wollen ist ein Etwas-Wollen."—Peters, *Willenswelt*, p. 126. See too p. 236, on Von Hartmann's statement of the same principle.

what we ought rather to say is, that outside of any system—in a region which the understanding cannot reach—there dwells in each of us a power called will. It is the working power of the self, and like the self it is a mystery which transcends thought.

Such are the conditions and such the contents of our self-consciousness. What we know both of ourselves and of our power of work has in it a mystical element of the utmost certainty as a fact, and yet an insoluble puzzle to the understanding. And this mysterious part of us is not far away. It is, to borrow a Scripture expression, very nigh us in our mouth and in our heart. The self which stands distinguished from all material things, the will which has not yet entangled itself with any of the fettering conditions of action, are the self and the will with which in our immediate life we have to do.

But is there any practical use in thinking of the mystery of our nature?

26. But even if this be conceded, a question may still be raised as to the practical necessity or usefulness of thinking of the mystery within ourselves. It might be the nearest thing to us, and all action might depend on it; but it still

might be a kind of unvarying element in life which nothing we can do will make less or more; like the atmosphere, which is indeed the most powerful and indispensable agency in keeping things in their place, but which, because it is so constantly and closely present, does not practically require to be thought of. We know, it may be said, that the self within us cannot stir, cannot make itself known even to itself without using the bodily and mental powers with which it stands in such a strange and inexplicable connection; and these bodily and mental powers form part of the system of nature. May we not spend our time better in learning what we can about these indispensable instruments of the inner self, and about the conditions under which they must be exercised, than in troubling ourselves about that central mystery which must ever remain a mystery to us?

27. It is indeed of immense importance to acquaint ourselves with the laws of our state and life. It is of the same moment for us to do so that it is *We must learn the laws of our life which operate independently of our wills;* for a workman to know the tools with which he has to labour and the materials on which he

has to work. If we forget that we are servants to law, and refuse to learn the terms of our service, we shall very speedily be called to bitter account for the omission. It is not only in the outward world, but in the inward that we find ourselves subjects and not masters. Our very intellect itself works not according to our will but independently of it, and often contrary to it. We may mark alike in the extremes of intellectual weakness and of intellectual strength the fact that the intellect is but an unmanageable and intractable, although very powerful, instrument of the inner self.

How often in hours of weakness do the thoughts wander in spite of the will? It is not merely that occasional imaginations present themselves, suggested by some external object, the presence of which is quite independent of any exercise of our mind; but trains of thought are pursued in order and sequence, while all the time we had infinitely rather the whole were banished from our minds. The mind seems to behave altogether like a piece of machinery, working away in spite of the unskilled overseer who has lost the secret of stopping it. The humiliation which wandering thoughts inflict upon our conceit of self-mastery is a common subject of complaint. And to represent the fact in its true proportion we must recognise not only our liability to distractions in our trains of thought, but the great insubordination of our trains of thought themselves to the command of our will.

This species of inward rebellion may be supposed to be felt most by minds which are weak or enervated through want of discipline. But when we turn to minds of the totally opposite character, we are no less struck by the resemblance of the mind to a machine which does its work by self-action independently of the will. The discoveries, and inventions, and productions of genius which form the triumphs of human intellect are attained by concentrated thought. But does the discoverer will that his thought shall work out his discovery? That would imply that he knew beforehand what it was to be. The thought comes to him he knows not whence or how, according to laws of the mind which he did not frame, and which operate by no power of his will. This, however humbling to our pride it may be, is the condition on which we hold our intellects, and this is all we can know about these wonderful instruments in possession of which we are placed. We ought to learn what they are capable of, to keep them in good order, and set them in motion; they will then work of themselves.

28. But the only reason why it should be worth our while to know anything at all about our intellects is found in the supposition that we have some power to command their operation. If they were really in every way independent of our will there would be as little practical use in learning what they can do or how they can be kept in order as the railway traveller finds in knowing the construction of the engine by which he is whirled along, or, perhaps we should say, as the engine finds for knowing its own construction. It is because we are not only the machine but also owners and guides of the machine, that it is necessary we should know its laws. Some years ago a clever physician, Dr. Henry Maudsley, published a book of much interest upon the power of the mind itself to prevent insanity. He proved how much in madness is due to physical causes, and how preventable they are. He showed how

but there would be no use in learning them if we had no power to guide them.

many phenomena which appear to be purely mental are in truth material. But when all was said there was one thing which he had not effected. He had not brought into the line of physical sequence that power within men to which he appealed when he called upon them to observe his rules. If he had done so he would have at once reduced his own work to an absurdity; for why should men be asked either to bring about or to prevent that which by the laws of nature must happen? He proved that people go mad through physical causes just as surely as a clock goes wrong when its works are allowed to rust. But this becomes useful to know only when we grant that there is an owner of the instrument endowed with power and responsibility for keeping it in order.

Very lately the same author has produced a work entitled *Body and Will*, in which he accumulates proofs of the dependence of the human mind upon material conditions. But it is impossible for him to state the terms of the problem without introducing considerations inconsistent with his own materialism. For instance, in proving the absolute dependence of the will on motives, he reminds us that punishments are inflicted upon law breakers, "under the tacit implication that the will is not an undetermined power, but that it may be influenced by motive to act this way or that."[1] Now to maintain that the will "may be influenced to act this way or that" is to grant that the will *is* an undetermined power. A determined power is one which must act in this way alone, and not in this way or that. Again, the author inquires "if a man must patiently manufacture himself to habits of well-doing by the diligent practice of doing well, and on most occasions perceives good habits to be a better security of good conduct than good principles, what becomes of the opinion that free will is the foundation and fountain of morality?"[2] And he conceives that he disposes of the necessity of free will to moral responsibility by suggesting that perhaps "a man's responsibility is not for doing what he does, being what he is, but for being what he is." But if the conditions of human nature and the power of habits stand opposed to free will in respect of particular acts, why do they not stand opposed to free will in

---

[1] *Body and Will*, by Henry Maudsley, M.D., p. 8.
[2] *Ibid.* p. 94.

respect of the acquisition of habits themselves? Responsibility for being what he is is just the same kind of thing as responsibility for doing what he does. "Were any man really free he would be free from responsibility for his character, which he could not then train and fashion." Yes; but were any man really not free he could not train and fashion his character. But in truth this clever book has for its radical vice a forgetfulness of one "obvious reflection" which the author himself makes: "Everything which we know is a synthesis of subject and object."[1] Now it will be found that throughout the work the subject is systematically excluded from consideration, and the materials and laws of that part of the world which is the object of our knowledge fill the whole field of view.[2]

[1] *Body and Will*, by Henry Maudsley, M.D., p. 45.

[2] The same may be said of the reasoning of Mr. Pollock (*Spinoza*, p. 190-1), in which he considers himself to have proved that the division of subject and object is identical with that of matter and mind. These writers have fallen into the error described by Professor Ferrier:

"The *ego* comes before us along with whatever comes before us. Hence we are familiar with it to an excess. We are absolutely surfeited with its presence. Hence we almost entirely overlook it. We attend to it but little. That neglect is inevitable. Its perpetual presence is almost equivalent to its perpetual absence."—*Institutes of Metaphysic*, p. 200.

29. Owners of machinery do indeed make fatal mistakes when they suppose that the laws by which their engines work will be governed by their wishes; and it is a similar and equally serious error for men to forget that the laws of the universe work within their own nature as well as around it, or to imagine that those laws can be induced to vary their operation according to the will of man. And no doubt it is an error which is habitually committed. Men imbue those bodies and minds which are the instruments of life with habits of intemperance, or sensuality, or indolence. And they promise themselves in despite of all experience that at some future time, when they please so to do, they will cast these off in a moment, and will to be—and actually be—all that they now perceive they ought to be. They forget that however free the will may be in itself, its power to produce effects even within the body and mind with which it is immediately connected is limited by the circumstances and conditions of the case, the most important of which are found in the state of those organs of body and of mind with which it must needs work. They manufacture

Two common errors:
1. *neglect of the laws of being;*
2. *neglect of the power of the will which is independent of law.*

for themselves conditions of body and of circumstances so sternly requiring the continuance of their miserable habits, that their wills find the difficulty too great ever to make the effort which at a distance seemed so easy and so sure. This is a familiar topic with the moralist—a warning often repeated in vain, as the graves of too many slaves to their own evil habits sadly testify.

And yet when the moralist has been dwelling as strongly as he can upon the bondage which closes upon those who deliver themselves over to sin, his mind misgives him that he is omitting an opposite truth of even greater importance, namely, the power of the will to contend with habits, with circumstances, with laws, and to overcome. It is easy for the onlooker to say that whatever power the will exerts must come from habit, law, and circumstance; but that is not the point of view in which those who determine to be free must consider the matter. If they think of it thus their will is paralysed, and they refuse to make the effort of which, could they have brought themselves to it, they were perfectly capable. Dr. Maudsley urges that much of Saul the Jew goes into the formation of Paul the Christian. We need not deny it; but if this argument displays to us a Paul bound by all his former history, another view shows us with as great truth a Paul bound by nothing in his former history. And the latter is the view which it was by far the most needful for Paul to take. And he did take it, for his motto was "I will not be brought under the power of any." The power of habits and of circumstances is perfectly well known to us. It gives us notice, however unwilling we be to accept notice, of the dominion which it is going to exert over us. But of how much is that energy capable which issues from those secret depths of our nature of which the causes and the operations do not lie open to the observation even of ourselves. Even against mighty odds, and with damaged and imperfect faculties for its instruments, it is hard to say what this mysterious energy may not effect if once it puts itself forth. Many cases have been known in which all scientific calculation as to the motives which will guide a man, or as to the powers which he can evolve, have been utterly falsified by some reaction of his inward self against the captivity brought upon him by his own very acts. This is what we call power of will. We must call it by this name and believe in it if we wish to reap the benefit of it. We must recognise it as consisting not in physical or intellectual qualities, but in energies that have their source beyond the reach of observation and thought.

30. The battle of life resembles literal warfare in many ways; but in nothing more than this, that you find some soldiers who gain their victories by the excellence of their weapons, and some whose success must be ascribed to their essential manliness; while the perfect soldier combines both. Peculiar powers of intellect and peculiar directions of taste resemble weapons which the will has at its disposal. And as nations must ever be trying to improve their arms both of assault and defence, and must learn that no courage will give victory without good weapons, and that no care can be too great to be expended on their manufacture, so must every man determine to improve to the utmost the powers and opportunities with which he has been endowed. Yet the weapons and the warrior are very distinguishable, and it is in vain that they are improved if he remains a coward; perhaps the more a coward because of the attention which he pays to his arms and of the grand show which

The self is the warrior: the talents are his weapons.

they make. The illustration may seem inappropriate to the case in which the mental and bodily powers which we compare to weapons, and the self and will which we compare to the warrior, alike lie within the constitution of a man. We grant the fact; the mystery of human nature consists in this. But it is as certain and as practical a truth to say that the bodily and mental powers are separable from the essential man as to say that the weapons and the warrior are different.

Many men are successful in the world and make great conquests in the intellectual domain of whom you can only pronounce that their talents are great. Tasks are easy to them which are difficult or impossible to others. They may be hard workers, but they never would have become such if delight in congenial and successful labour had not drawn them on. It is by aptitude and not by will that they grow great. And just as behind the glittering armour of a mediæval knight a poor creature enough might hide, so behind the talents of many a man of fame there may be an inner self of very inferior quality. Though he be as proud of his talents and think them as truly his own as conceited persons think their money or their clothes, yet, in truth, his gifts are as separable from his true self as garments or wealth; and he has no more right to pride himself on them than his purse-proud neighbour has to glory in his inherited possessions. Nor is this unfelt by other men. Very often, persons never heard of in the great world, and whose talents are slender, produce on those who know both well the impression of a larger being than that of the gifted individual who despises them.

31. Talents may be improved by education; as well by the education of early years when wise preceptors watch and develop the bent of a child's powers, as by that of later times when people undertake their own education and continue it as the great task of their lives. *Education of the talents and education of the will.* But wise preceptors of youth and wise self-teachers are alike aware that there is such a thing as developing the talents without developing the central man, and dealing with the mind without dealing with the soul. When a man has learnt this, neither fame, nor wealth, nor success, nor even that better thing of which fame and success should be the stamp—

namely, matured power and conscious mental strength—will satisfy him so long as he must feel that the self which is nearer to him than his fame or even his talents, remains unperfected. And it is not more certain that the talents can be improved than that the inner self may be strengthened.

How to strengthen it is the question which is better worth asking and better worth answering than any other that life can raise. It cannot be answered in a self-satisfied spirit or by any who refuse to recognise the mystery of life. Faith in ourselves is our great need; that faith which dispenses with sight and is a kind of religion. But even talents need aid from without to assist their development, and those who refuse to be helped are little likely to make the best of their abilities; and dependence is still more plainly our condition in the affairs of the soul. It is a mysterious region. We cannot understand it. It is ourselves, yet more than anything in our life it leads us beyond ourselves. The possession of this mysterious personality and will makes us powerful and independent of circumstances for every task of life to a degree that we ourselves cannot measure. But it also renders us dependent, we cannot tell how far, upon those incomprehensible powers which are akin to the mystery within ourselves. Where to find such powers, how to turn them to our use, and how to apply the mysterious endowments of our own nature in relation to them, is the subject which we have next to consider.

III.

KNOWLEDGE OF MEN.

"As in water face answereth to face, so the heart of man to man."
—Prov. xxvii. 19.

32. WE are putting but an imaginary case when we suppose a man perfectly conscious of his own nature, with its wants and problems, looking out into the world to see what help he can there find in his self-development. For, as matter of fact, our knowledge of the world and of the help it can give begins at the same time with our knowledge of ourselves, and we become conscious by equal steps of the problems of the outward world and of those which are found within. Still it is possible in thought to separate self and the outer world. When the period of mature reflection has come, our self-knowledge ranges itself close to

The self seeks help from the outer world. The mystery of the passage to it.

us, and our knowledge of other things and people lies beyond. And it is distinctly a step in advance, and one which requires to be well justified, when from belief in our own personality we proceed forward to the belief that any persons meet us in the region that lies beyond the castle walls of self.

It will evidently be unreasonable that we should deal with the outward world on principles which have been found inapplicable to the world of self. One who requires a kind of proof or evidence in the outer world which he has to do without in the inward, resembles the feudal lords who were sometimes known as lax and good-natured in the requirements they made of their own families, while they were strict and cruel in their demands upon their dependents. We have seen that we are incomprehensible to ourselves. However much we can understand about our life we cannot understand the central mystery which constitutes the true self. Like a horse trying to lick off a fly which is too near his mouth to allow him to touch it, we find that the part of ourselves which really lies closest to us is that part which is least comprehensible. But though it is incomprehensible we cannot put it aside as something of which we need not think. On the contrary, the incomprehensible self is that which is in constant use, and which refuses to be ignored. And thus, if we be wise, we go out into the world in a humble frame, and ready to accept truth which is forced on us by practical experience or irresistible feeling without being able to understand it.

And indeed we cannot make a single step out of our own door without finding occasion to exercise this temper. The very passage to the outward world is itself full of mystery and question. How can we know that anything is without, when we plainly know only by means which are within our frame? Like Rebecca in the story describing to the disabled knight what she sees out of the window, so our senses inform our mind of what they find beyond. But the mind cannot accept their information without great misgivings. It feels that the senses have no powers capable of explaining the nature of the things of which they tell. How shall it assure itself that there is anything at all outside corresponding to what they report? And yet on the other hand it seems impossible to imagine in ourselves a power of seeing and hearing that which appears to be real, and at the same time a power of looking behind the mirror and finding out that what seemed to be real is not real at all. In the long run the existence of a world is a mystery which must be accepted but accepted without being understood.

33. Let us suppose this first great difficulty surmounted, and that we are well out into the open, with the firm ground of a known world under our feet. We by no means find that the acceptance of one great mystery at the bidding of instinct has completed the humiliations to which the understanding must submit, or the list of occasions on which it must hand over the office of guide to humbler faculties. Why the particles of which the material world is composed came together to form it, and why coming together they still do not cease to be separable particles; how forces act and how motion is produced—what have we to say in answer to these questions but "I cannot tell"? And yet the cohesion and the separability of atoms is part of the necessary knowledge we have of the world. We cannot

Mystery of matter. Mystery of life. Mystery of intelligence.

dispense with the fact that this is the character of matter. Neither can we understand it. It is a mystery which we are forced to recognise and use. We cannot ignore it; but we can very easily forget that it is a mystery, and complacently imagine that because it is familiar it is also understood.

When living creatures come under our notice we receive in addition to the wide enlargement of our interests and the helps of life which they bring to us, a large accession also to the stock of truth which we must receive but cannot understand. What is life, and how does it arise? What is sensation—that strange phenomenon which we observe in living creatures, and upon which their interest and use for us so entirely depends? Even if we could understand the impact of one body on another, and how they come together and yet remain separate, we should still be unable to understand how in the case of living beings there is not merely an impact but an impression. There is a certain kind of effect or result to the living creature from the presence of an external object, wholly different from what would have followed had the creature not been alive. There is an indescribable and incomprehensible something within the living being that receives the external presence in a way in which dead matter could not have received it, and adds to the material results of the meeting a phenomenon quite beyond our understanding, which we call sensation.

But when from inanimate things and from the lower creatures we pass on to men we find ourselves in the presence of accumulated wonders. Even were we able to understand sensation in itself, how shall we understand the process by which sensations are taken in, and so connected and distinguished, and manipulated by something within, which men call their mind, as to turn them into knowledge?[1] The experience of sensations no more accounts for knowledge than a field of corn accounts for a loaf of bread. The materials of knowledge we see given from without: nothing is

---

[1] "All the data of sense could give me no idea of objects, nay, could not even enable me to attain to that unity of consciousness which is necessary for the knowledge of myself as an object of inner sense . . . It is true, that if I make myself in thought a pure animal, I can conceive these sensible ideas as carrying on their regular play in my soul, seeing that they might still be bound together by an empirical law of association, and so have influence on feeling and desire . . . but then I should not through these ideas have knowledge of anything, even of my own state."—Kant, quoted by Caird (*Philosophy of Kant*, p. 266).

in the intellect which was not first in the sense. We are well aware that if shut in from contact with the external world the mind of man could no more think or know than a mill could move without wind or grind without corn. But the wonder is that though the dependence of man upon the outward world for his mental stores appears so complete, yet what comes forth from him as knowledge of the outward world is a great deal more than that which we have seen the outward world bring to him. In the process of passing through the mind sensations are wonderfully transmuted by powers, within which work with all possible regularity and decision, and which constitute the very basis of man's mental life. And yet they are extremely mysterious. Watch a child which is making its first acquaintance with the world of things. You will see that the process is not like the introduction of furniture into an uninhabited house, where the place for everything has to be chosen and things might as well be put in one part as in another. Rather it resembles the furnishing of a house which is made so ready for the process that everything as it comes is caught up by active servants and set in a place assigned and adapted for it among surroundings already provided, and which make it look quite different from the article which was delivered at the door.

To what degree the preparation which is somehow in the mind already, though latent and unawakened, mingles with even the most elementary perceptions that come to us from the outside world, it is very hard to say. These original possessions of the mind itself are precisely those which it is most difficult for the mind to disengage and to describe. We cannot be sure that any sensation whatever, even in its most elementary form, is the same thing to men which it is to the inferior creatures. But great metaphysical subtlety and close thinking are required to analyse the common every-day facts of our intercourse with the outside world, and to show how much in the impressions which they produce and in the message which they deliver to us is due to outward things themselves, and how much to the powers of the intellect and to general conceptions and habits of working either involved in the very essence of the mind or inherited in some strange way from previous generations. It has been shown to the conviction of a great number of thinkers that the framing in place and time without which no picture of the outer world can ever find a place in our conception is not furnished from without, but after the entrance of the originating sensation into the mind. But what are these conceptions of space and time without which we can have no ideas of anything, yet which no external object brings into our minds? And what are we to call that power of the mind which possesses them? We cannot tell: things can only be known as in space and time, but space and time can only be known in connection with things. Nor do we know the mysterious power of the mind from which they come except in its power of connecting and arranging the stores contributed by the senses. Mysterious though the power be, yet there is no doubt that if we did not possess it our perceptions would hang loose and unconnected and quite unworthy of the name of knowledge.

34. Mathematical science affords an example which is evident to us all, of something added by *Mystery of truth.* a mysterious power within to the experience which comes through our intercourse with the outside world. The mind is plainly not independent of sensible experience

even with respect to mathematical science. That is to say, a mind, if such were imaginable, cut off from all sensation and all contact with what lies without, could never have conceived from stores of its own the notions of numbers or of figures. It could never have counted one, two, three, or imaged a line, a circle, or a square. But in so far as counting things that are before the eyes or before the imagination — in so far as acquiring by experience the ideas of shapes and forms and retaining the notions thus acquired in the memory, there seems nothing peculiarly strange: and the understanding is able to follow the process, though with the same incompleteness that it it finds in all its experience. But in all matters of pure experience the understanding strictly forbids us to imagine that our experience is necessarily common to all minds. It tells us that to derive universal or necessary notions from our experience is the very mark of childishness or savagery, and is the greatest possible contradiction of experience itself, which constantly shows us how narrow and imperfect our experience is. And though when our experience happens to be confirmed by that of a great many other persons in a large number of instances, and with none to the contrary, we at last arrive at the conviction that we have reached what we call a law of nature, yet we can never feel sure by mere observation that this law of nature obtains throughout the universe, nor even if we did, could we know that it not only *is* but *must be* so. It is part of the uniform course of nature that fire burns. But can any one lay down as a fact that fire burns everywhere throughout the universe? Even if you were in a position to do this, can you be sure that fire not only does but must burn, and that it could not do otherwise in any place or circumstances whatever? We cannot say so. But when we arrive at a mathematical truth this is the very thing that we do say. A conviction that it is universally true and cannot under any circumstances be otherwise accompanies our very perception of it. And thus we have a kind of knowledge which springs out of experience and yet bears a fruit entirely beyond experience. In the course of its development it disengages itself from the material facts in which it had its beginning: it rules experience, and not experience it. Its definitions express something which never was and never will be exactly embodied in matter, for they are too exact for coarse material bodies to exemplify. No experiments in the material world are needed to prove its principles. But they are supreme over matter and thought alike. And we are incapable of conceiving or of believing in the existence of any mind or any world for which they shall not be valid.

Consider, then, our progress in knowledge. In our very first experience of an external world we find not merely that there is much we do not know, but that in the very centre of what we do know there is a mysterious element, a certain and indispensable truth which is as incomprehensible as it is certain. When we proceed further to consider the phenomena of sensation, we find other facts which are equally certain yet as impossible to be understood. When we think of human beings and their acquisition of knowledge we find powers developed in them which no previous facts suffice to account for: mysterious powers, yet undoubtedly real. And when we observe the human mind reaching to necessary truth and knowing not merely what is, but what must be, we reach a further stage in that progress by which knowledge of the most certain kind springs and grows up we know not how.

35. It is hardly possible for any one who considers this progress in knowledge and the nature of it to avoid the conclusion that along with the outward world and through it we are all in contact with a source of thoughts and convictions which lies beyond the world, and which the understanding, capable as it is only of dealing with the sequence of earthly facts, cannot comprehend. When we say that an unknowable element enters into all knowledge, we assert a truth, but not the whole truth. The point is that this unknowable is not wholly unknowable. It enters into our knowledge and makes part of it. It assumes various forms to us, and there is a progress in what it teaches.

<small>We must be in contact with a source of knowledge beyond the sensible world. The perception of beauty.</small>

We are only proceeding forward on the same lines when we trace the operation of a teaching which comes from beyond the senses in our ideas of beauty and of right as we have found it in our ideas of truth. So varied is this unknowable in its form that it meets us everywhere and in every kind of knowledge, whether it be of that kind which is definite or that which is felt more than stated: for as Goethe says, " It is not always necessary that truth must be incorporated. It is sometimes enough if it hovers around us and brings us into harmony with itself: if, like the sound of bells with solemn friendly tone, it lingers in the air."

Those who have felt most deeply the sense of beauty, and thought most deeply upon its nature, have recognised this spiritual character in it. What is it that speaks to the mind in art and in nature? If a primrose by a river's brim be to a man a yellow primrose and nothing more, the poet tells us that such a man does not feel its beauty. And yet what *is* the yellow primrose more than a yellow primrose? Neither the senses nor yet the understanding can tell what. "A spirit far more deeply interfused" mingles with all nature and communicates to us a message of beauty which refuses to be weighed and measured by the intellect, and vanishes if the intellect presses its questions too far. Not but what this beauty is of the nature of truth. Truth in art is the first requisite of beauty: and the beauty of nature, from which that of art is derived, has ever in it a something which we feel to be allied to truth. We regard it as a reproof to anything false or wicked in ourselves, and it seems to us far more excusable that men should be evil in the midst of the ugliness of great cities than among beautiful scenes of nature. There is a strict connexion between beauty and truth, and the principles of beauty can even be in some degree reduced to rules which may be studied and found useful in the comprehension or production of what is beautiful. But the basis of beauty lies beyond all rules, and cannot be understood.

36. And the same character belongs to our moral being. In the history of the development of conscience there is no doubt that much is to be attributed to the influence of social laws. But when all has been granted that can be proved—one had almost said that can be asked—by the extremest advocates of evolution in morals, something remains behind. Even if we traced all morality to the growth of social laws, yet in that original capacity of human nature for social intercourse which gives their power to such laws, we must acknowledge something for which materialism does not account; in other words, an

The perception of right.

infusion of the supernatural. And however much we attribute to development we must recognise that original infusion of the supernatural as accompanying the whole process; and we cannot separate the power of conscience from connexion with it. Whoever recognises in conscience only social law in the earthly aspect of law, rejects its most commanding part. We need no more deny the power which the progress of human history and experience has had upon the development of moral, than that which they have had upon mathematical, science. But in the one case as in the other, the earthly history is made the channel of a power which is more than earthly. Conscience speaks to us not merely with the sanction of expediency proved through past generations, but also with a mysterious force which invests the duties imposed by earthly circumstances with an authority that earth could never have given.

Such is our mental wealth, and so it flows in upon us. If we determine that we can know nothing except that which we can fully understand, we shall have to reject not merely the highest and noblest but even the surest, thoughts and feelings of which our minds are capable. But indeed what is mysterious in our knowledge is but the natural counterpart of the mystery that is in ourselves. When we have apprehended how certain it is that each of us is a separate self, and yet how incomprehensible it is that we should be anything more than a part of nature, we are prepared for those intimations of truths and realities beyond nature which reach us in spite of our bondage to the senses, as glimpses of the sky might reach a prisoner between the walls which confine him.

37. This being our case in respect to our knowledge of ourselves and our knowledge of the world of things, we cannot approach the question of our knowledge of other men with the determination to recognise in them nothing but what we can perceive with the senses and understand with the intellect.

How then do we know other men?

It is certain indeed that but for our sensible experience we should be quite unaware of the existence of any other men in the world. Other men reach us through our sight, our hearing, our touch; and one deprived of these senses would be deprived of their company. We have understandings which combine and reduce to system the messages which our senses convey, and they deal with those experiences which bring us in contact with men as they do with all other experiences. Men appear as combinations of phenomena as much as stones and trees. The phenomena combined in them are more numerous and complicated, and are perhaps more widely varied in different cases than those of stones and trees; but the essential point is the same, that men appear to us as combinations of phenomena. And as curiosity and the desire to turn our observations to profit prompt us to learn the order in which phenomena in other combinations appear and disappear; so we are prompted in like manner to make systematic observations with regard to human beings and to combine them into scientific rules of action.

38. A very large and important part of our conduct towards men is framed upon the principle of attending the phenomena of human life and combining our observations. Children are reared and trained as plants are watered and tended. Similar treatment is expected to produce similar

Much of our knowledge of men comes from sensible observation.

effects upon the children as upon the plants. Great national measures of education and civilisation are expected to yield their proper returns, just as great measures of drainage and cultivation. Nay, so closely are the worlds of nature and of man connected, that the very processes of draining and clearing tracts of land are themselves looked to as sure to yield results equally definite and natural in the men who inhabit the country as in the plants that grow there. Nor will it be only in the physical part of man's constitution that these consequences will flow. The phenomena of his mental and even his moral life may be studied, and the conditions on which they rest discovered. And the sciences thus framed have proved full of fruitfulness. Physiology studies the nature of the individual man, and sociology that of man in society; and though both these sciences be very complicated and difficult there is no doubt that they are thoroughly well founded. In all this there is no mystery except the mystery which underlies all things alike: no special mystery in man different in kind from that which we notice in the lower creatures and in the vegetable world. There is a considerable difference in degree both in the number of observations required and in the wonder and interest of the pursuit. Yet it is only a difference in degree. Natural history is a fascinating subject. Both plants and animals of the lower kinds awaken affection ; and the study of mankind might be granted to be only the highest kind of natural history without thereby proving it impossible to feel both an interest in the science and love for the subjects of it equal to the splendid results which we derive from its pursuit.

39. But is this all? If it be all, then other men are not as we. For in ourselves, besides the unvarying and unbroken series of physical causes producing their physical effects, there is a mysterious power *But the knowledge of their personality cannot come from that source.* which is not our body nor our intellects, nor any of the phenomena of these, nor any part of us that we can understand, but ourselves. Though we recognise in our own life a natural history, a physical series as closely linked as any that we can see going on anywhere around us, yet in us this is not all ; it is not the chief thing, the reason why we are ourselves. It is the mystery behind, that enables us to say "I myself," and that is the ground of our self-consciousness ; and this

alone enables us to call our faculties our own, instead of observing them as a part of the machinery of nature at large.

Are we then to say that it is we ourselves alone who possess this personality? Is each one to himself the only person in the universe, recognising in his own case that I myself which is not a combination of his faculties but the owner of them all, but able to discern in other men nothing but faculties, or perhaps we should rather say nothing but a series of natural causes producing their natural effects?

This would be a position of things very different from that which ordinary language and men's common way of thinking assume. For in their language and thought the sharpest distinction is made between persons and things, and we are supposed to be conversant with both in our daily life. A system which should regard all other human beings as mere series of phenomena would place them in the kingdom of things, not of persons, and out of that kind of correspondence with ourselves which we call personal. On this supposition the distinction in kind between things living and things dead seems to vanish, and the one appears the subject of outward influences not less completely than the other. The distinction in kind between consciousness and unconsciousness loses its significance; for consciousness is on this supposition nothing but an impotent witness of a series of events which proceeds without allowing it any right of interference.

40. Now there is, as we have already allowed, a great deal to be said in support of such a system. There is no doubt whatever that very large departments of human life as we observe it in our fellow-men fall necessarily into nature, and present themselves as part of the invariable and unchangeable series of physical causation. What part of man as we observe him can be excepted from physical causation? Not his body; for that falls under the operation of physical law just as much as any other mass of matter in the system of nature. Nor yet his mind. The intellect cannot be exempted from the operation of law any more than the body, which in all its changes is so plainly subject to it. We have found this to be the case with our own bodies and minds, which work often without our will, sometimes in

The knowledge of man as a department of natural history.

spite of our will, and always by powers which our will can only influence but never originate; and the same is the case with others. In our case we found no refuge from the conclusion that self and will are words which express no meaning at all, or a delusive one, except in our consciousness that self and will are realities—a consciousness which has palpable outward effects in human action, and is implied in our feelings and our language with a strength which is able to maintain itself against any arguments. Arguments must address themselves to the powers of the human mind, and there is no power in the human mind which more essentially belongs to it than the consciousness of will and of self. The way is barred against any argument tending to overthrow this consciousness, for sheer want of any tribunal within us whose determinations have any greater validity than the consciousness in question possesses.

We cannot have the consciousness of the personality of other men which we have of our own. Are we then the only persons in existence?

41. However, this consciousness is by its very nature incapable of being communicated to anybody else with the same force which it possesses for the mind of its owner. Men have it of themselves but they cannot have it of other

men.[1] When we have catalogued the palpable and cognisable facts of other men's constitution: the powers, bodily and mental, of which facts have proved them to be possessed: the tendencies which experience has shown in them, and the necessities which their surroundings impose, we have said all that our minds can directly know about them. They tell us, indeed, that they also like ourselves, feel that there is something more; they believe themselves endowed with free will and with personality. But we cannot be sure from any observed facts that this is not a delusion on their part. Although we find it plainly worth our while to humour them in this notion, and to deal with them as if they possessed this free will which they claim, yet we know that there are many other notions which pass for true in the intercourse of society without being genuine facts.

---

[1] "When I look at another man I do not perceive his consciousness. I see only a compound body of a certain form or colour moving in this or that manner. I do not immediately know that he perceives, feels, and thinks, as I do myself. He may be an exquisitely formed puppet, requiring perhaps more mechanical skill in the construction than ever has been attained by man, but still a mere machine. When I attribute to him personality and consciousness, I mediately and reflectively transfer to another that of which I am directly cognisant only in myself."—Mansel, *Prolegomena Logica*, p. 140.

And, indeed, we constantly detect an undeniable mixture of delusion in men's persuasion that they possess a free self. We find them habitually overrating the power which their will possesses over their physical nature. They think that they will do so or so: but we who have calmly considered their organism, and estimated the future results to which their past tends, foresee with confidence that they will do nothing of the kind. And we, not they, turn out in a great many cases to be right. We ask ourselves, what if this were the whole account of the matter; and if their supposition that they are individual selves and possess wills were total delusion? And we must reply that in that case the last sign of any external personality goes down beneath the current of natural law, and we look forth upon the unbroken and ceaseless flow of things, ourselves the only persons in existence.

Whatever evidences of personality in mankind may be urged in answer to this conclusion, will be found as imperfect in their own way as evidences of the being of God or of the truth of Christianity have ever been in theirs. The utmost that such treatises can effect in their sphere is to produce a probability; to adduce facts which are most reasonably accounted for on the supposition of the truth in question; to remove objections, and make the way of belief intellectually open to those whose instincts lead them to believe. But there must ever remain ways of escape from belief for those who have not the instinct of belief. The facts may always be possibly accounted for on another hypothesis. And if the mind comes to the examination prejudiced in favour of the contrary hypothesis, the facts fall naturally into their place under it. Thus it is with the hypothesis of human personality. When we argue the question with ourselves whether the men around us are really persons, or whether they are the mere productions of circumstances and the action of material forces, we are not able to advance any arguments convincing to our intellects why the former theory should be accepted rather than the latter. All we can prove is that, from some points of view, things look strangely like their personality; that if they have not genuine will, material forces have assumed forms wonderfully like to genuine will. But material forces in their numberless complications are doubtless capable of assuming very strange forms, and this may be one of them.

42. We must bring to the aid of the lagging arguments for human personality the recognition of an instinct or a feeling which draws us towards other persons, and knows them as such. Of this instinct no account can be given to the mind; it can but recognise the fact that we possess the instinct. We have already seen in how many departments of thought and feeling we appear possessed of powers which work inevitably, but of the working of which the mind can give no explanation. In mathematics, æsthetics, morals, the highest and best part of every conviction is found in a super-sensible element which the intellect accepts and registers, but of which it can furnish no account to itself. And why should not the same be the case in man's knowledge of man? There seems nothing wonderful in asserting that while man can understand a great deal about his brother man, the highest and best part of that brother, his personality, is something which is given to him as a datum which his mind is to accept, and not as an acquisition of the mind. He cannot

There must be an instinct in us for recognising persons as mysterious as our personality itself.

refuse to accept it, but it declines to be made an object of his science.

43. In the departments of mathematics, æsthetics, and morals alike, there is a great difference in the use which different men make of the principles which are given to their minds. We cannot believe that there are any men absolutely destitute of all feeling of the truth on which these sciences are founded. They would be less than men if they were. But it is certain that different men give very different degrees of supremacy within them to the truth or the beauty or the righteousness which they must perceive in some degree, even though dimly; and that they work it out in practice with very different degrees of completeness. So that to some men the spiritual and eternal element would seem almost to vanish out of all these departments, and nothing to remain but combinations of earthly ideas; while to others earthly facts seem only starting-places and occasions of very little account in themselves for the introduction of thoughts and feelings that pass altogether beyond earthly expression. And so it seems to be with man's knowledge of man

Different men have different degrees of belief in the personality of other men.

Personality in our brother man is not a fact which is recognised equally and of course by all men. There are some who both profess to believe in it and act up to the profession: and some whose recognition of it in practice is far less real than that which they pretend to. And there may be others so far led by the arguments against human personality as to deny it in theory, but whose practical recognition of it, in spite, as it were, of themselves, is very strong indeed. And last and lowest of all, there are many men who scarcely even profess to regard their brother men as differing in any essential point from the inanimate world, and who practically treat them altogether as things.

The temper which produces the latter state of mind is rightly called selfishness. A man realises intensely his own self. He tries to forget or to ignore whatever in the conditions of his life refuses to be subject to self. Self is the centre from which everything radiates. With such dispositions it is impossible for him to make that instinctive transfer of self into other men which enables us to realise them as possessed of the same personality that we have. They are confounded with the rest of the objects which surround the man and are to him simply part of that which is not himself. And the object which he sets before him is to make everything else the instrument of self and subject to its will. There is, it is well known, a very possible and even common condition of mind which regards all human beings as mere tools and ministers of selfishness. And it is also a fact, admitted and experienced, that whoever treats other men in this way will degrade instead of elevating that self of his own to which he sacrifices them. He loses the exercise of his own personality by ignoring theirs. He destroys, by refusing them the place of equal companions to himself, the appointed means by which his sense of his own freedom should be stimulated and developed. And by a paradox, strange and yet most certain, those who care most for self are those in whom self becomes thoroughly subjected and enslaved to external influences. "He that saveth his life shall lose it, and he that loseth his life for my sake, the same shall save it." So said the Son of Man: and it is in accordance with the whole spirit of His teaching that what He says of our relations to Himself should in a degree be true of those we hold to every human being about us, and of our general connexion with the whole human race. By losing ourselves in them we find ourselves: by intensely realising other men's personality we come to a sense of our own.

Even where there is nothing which we can call absolute selfishness there is a certain apathy towards the personality of our fellow men, which fails to realise what they are and what they may be to us. And this also reacts upon our sense of our own personality, and makes it indolent and even dead. But what seems more strange is that there are even ways of doing men good and of practising what we imagine to be love to them, which nevertheless regard them merely as things and passive subjects of physical law, missing all true hold upon their personality. It is not every kind of interest in mankind, or every kind of love to them, which is personal interest and love. A plant is more interesting than a stone, and a beast than a plant, but all are things, and we do not regard any of them as persons. It is common for men to describe their feeling towards inanimate things or towards the lower animals as love, and there is, as we have before remarked, much in the feeling which deserves that name. It is easy to see, therefore, that there may be a feeling towards mankind which may be called interest or even love, yet which does not truly regard them as persons, and differs only in degree, but not in kind, from that which is experienced towards the world of things.

44. And this seems to be a way of dealing with mankind which is peculiarly prevalent in these times. The scientific spirit of the age leads most thinkers to dwell upon that part of man's constitution by which he is in the system of nature than on that part by which he stands above nature. *Men may be regarded like things even by those who are trying to do them good.* In this point of view man's relationship to the other phenomena of the world can be laid down in a plausible manner, and his development can be made matter of science. His history can be represented as ruled by laws equally invariable with those which govern the life of plants and that of beasts. Many strange phenomena, it is true, present themselves in the history of man testifying in a way which partakes of the nature of miracle to the presence in every life of an element which cannot

be clearly brought under physical law, and which seems to bear witness to free will. But it is found possible to pass such symptoms by. They may be ascribed to the difficulties of the subject and the complicated way in which laws operate. And so in the view of many men mystery disappears from human nature, and physical law everywhere prevails.

While science is thus busy on the one side in reducing man to a part of nature, it is occupied on another in discoveries which tend to benefit his condition. They are discoveries of laws in the physical world, unknown before. It is because they are not occasional phenomena, but constantly recurring operations of law, that it is so good to learn them. If it was not known that they can be thoroughly depended on not to fail there would be little use in knowing them; but because they are unvarying laws man can bring them systematically into the service of his life, or his life into relations with them. These discoveries of physical law are useful to man only because he himself in part of his constitution belongs to the same department. He himself has powers, and wants, and desires, as regularly recurring and as well deserving the title of laws of nature as those physical phenomena by which they are helped and supplied. He must be a part of nature in order to derive benefit from his knowledge of natural laws. And a part of it he undoubtedly is, in a degree sufficient to enable him to respond constantly and invariably to improvements in the bearing upon him of the laws of external things.

When these discoveries in the regions of external nature are proceeding with energy and with brilliant results, and are found to yield fruit for the benefit of human life, while at the same time physical laws in the region of man's internal nature and history are searched out and proclaimed, it is no wonder that he should sometimes forget that there is anything but physical law in the world around him or in his own nature within. This is the more likely when the exclusive attention to such a law comes as a reaction from a condition of thought bearing the contrary character. In past times nature was thought to be governed, if not capriciously, yet by laws which admitted of constantly recurring exceptions. And an extravagant power in producing these exceptions—a power quite beyond what experience justifies—was ascribed to the human will, working by various methods, magical or otherwise. Then the chief known way of making men better and happier was by direct action on the human will. The attempt to improve the condition of large masses of mankind by removing physical impediments which lie in their way was not thought of. It was considered that if you could work upon man's own will he would be able to effect great things in overcoming natural disadvantages, and that even if he overcame none of them yet this would matter little if his own self reached its full development. Too little was known about the laws of nature and of human life to direct men's attention to those quarters, and man was dealt with in himself or left alone.

45. When we look back upon those old days with all their defects, their ignorance of the conditions of life, and their neglect of improvement in its surroundings, we cannot but sometimes feel that man as such was more to himself and to his brother man when nature was less. Even men who have themselves little spiritual belief have been struck by the tendency in modern life to

The present age in more danger of losing the recognition of personality than simpler times were.

reduce all people to the same model and abolish all true freedom of will and all individuality of character. But indeed how should men not be all of the same model, and why should they desire to be anything else if there be none but physical laws to govern them, and if those laws be always the same? We look with admiration upon discoveries which place mighty agencies of nature at the disposal of all men. We regard with sympathy attempts to abolish unnatural distinctions between man and man, and to spread to all men those benefits of nature which seem to belong as generally to all as the sun and the air. But as the benefits which scientific discoveries confer and those which flow from a scientific treatment of human life grow greater, men seem to lose the prophetic power of appeal to the central being of their brethren. All these great discoveries concern themselves not with men, but with things, or with men considered as things. They do not touch men as men. And the exclusive pursuit of them assimilates men to things. A vast and complicated system of nature is developed in our minds; it seems to include our brethren in it; but it hides their real selves from us. A barrier rises between them and us like that which separates us from the world of the lower animals.

Men let go the secret of coming heart to heart with one another when they think exclusively of the laws of nature. For these place us in no more real sympathy or brotherhood with man than with any other portion of that vast system of machinery of which all alike are parts. To appeal to man's secret nature, to approach him closely, to influence him, to love him in the truly human sense of that word, we must remember that mystical bond of personality which exists between him and us. Of this nature tells us nothing: but our own consciousness and the instincts which accompany consciousness tell us much.

46. We must not omit to learn the physical laws which govern our own external lives and those of our brethren. They are the conditions under which we live. If we neglect them, we neglect not only the opportunity of improvements in our external well-being, but also our true self-development. Man learns to know himself and finds his opportunities of self-improvement in

We must know the laws which govern other men's lives. But we must cultivate faith in them as persons.

his friendly contests with nature, where command can only be achieved on the condition of absolute obedience. We shall do little good either to ourselves or to other men by ignoring the physical laws among which we are set to live. If we are able to discover anything in nature ever so small which was not known before, or even to persuade men to better submission towards those natural laws which though known are not obeyed, we shall be benefactors to mankind, and superiority of knowledge and of service to human life will earn the gratitude of men. Yet when all this is done we may have acquired nothing of that which is properly called influence, the mysterious power which flows from person to person. We may be unable to teach any one how to make any of the discoveries we have revealed serviceable for the true elevation of self, which after all is the real man. And we and they together may resemble the ambitious seeker after a kingdom who lodges himself in a palace and clothes himself in purple only to find that in the midst of all he is unhealthy, old, and shrunken, and that his grand surroundings do him little good. We have forgotten those personal relations to each other which cannot be maintained without acknowledging a mystery: that mysterious recognition of self in others which corresponds to the mysterious self within.

Man's recognition of the personality of his fellow is a faith. It is in itself a kind of religion. We have to overpass sight in order to gain it. It is something which cannot be proved. But it is that on which depends all that is noblest and happiest in human life.

IV.

WE KNOW GOD THROUGH SELF-KNOWLEDGE.

"Man's goings are of the Lord; how can a man then understand his own way? . . . The spirit of man is the candle of the Lord, searching all the innermost parts of the belly."—PROV. xx. 24, 27.

47. THAT which makes ourselves to be ourselves, that which wills and acts in us, escapes our thought and baffles our powers of statement and description. We cannot define it; yet we cannot put it aside as something which does not concern us, except at the price of putting aside all life and action. It would be incorrect to suppose that this conviction is something which requires to be proved, or of which there can be any doubt. On the contrary, it is an obstinate and persistent fact of life which science has spent itself in arguing against for ages, now in this direction, now in that, but which

The mystery of personal life points to further mystery.

no amount of arguing has set aside, even for a moment. Men may indeed forget it, or hide it from themselves behind a mass of outward and visible facts which they observe and accumulate. But their whole system wants the breath of life, and when they open the valves through which the breath of life is admitted into the frame of man's mind and body, mystery comes in with it; mystery constitutes its very nature.

When we extend our view to our fellow men we find that personality in them can only be recognised on the condition that we are willing to accept a mystery. So long as they remain only things to us, so long we perceive no special mystery about them. But if we want to live with them as with persons, we can do so only by recognising in our own mysterious souls an instinctive power to discern other souls. Intercourse between men may be degraded far below this, into something merely of the same kind as the intercourse which man holds with the world. But the highest and best intercourse can only be founded on the faith which is willing to accept a mystery; and this is implicitly felt and acknowledged by all who have experience of the highest and best communion with other men. Every word we speak to a fellow man as to a being like ourselves is addressed to a mystery as truly as is prayer to God.

The belief in mystery is thus a practical necessity for man in his own life and in his intercourse with his fellows. Mystery is the word which seems best to express the facts of the case. The word denotes something known with the utmost certainty as a fact, but which cannot be understood in its causes, nor woven into a system with the facts which surround it. So long as a phenomenon can be ascribed to possible deception or mistake we do not speak of mystery, for deception and mistake are not mysterious but perfectly well known agencies. But when facts present themselves, and we become convinced that deception and mistake are words improper to be used of them, and they refuse, from any point of view, to disappear, we then pronounce that they are mysterious. And this is just the state of the case in respect of our own personality and that of other men. Mystery being thus admitted as a constituent ingredient in human life, and the faith which accepts and acts on mystery being recognised as demanded of us all by the common necessities of living, it is natural to ask whether the principle can be confined in its operation to human personalities, or whether the gap which is left open in the neatly-smoothed circuit of human science for the purpose of admitting this mystery is not large enough to admit other mysteries too.

48. When the city of Syracuse was besieged by the Athenians and the Spartans determined to send relief, it was believed by most in Greece that it was too late to save the town. It was thought that all that could now be done was to hover round the city and transport any stragglers who might escape, to some other settlements, where they might console themselves as they could for the loss of their homes. For the impression prevailed that the Athenians, a people extremely well skilled in sieges, had drawn their lines so completely round the place that no communication was any longer possible between the garrison and their friends outside. But when the relieving force came close enough to know the exact condition of things it was found that this was not the case. Although the lines had been drawn closely round

Science and mystery.

the larger portion of the town, yet one point remained which was still open. And through this little vacant space came the aid from without which in the end turned the hopes of the besiegers to defeat.

The city in this parable, as in Bunyan's *Holy War*, represents man's soul. The communication between the city and its friends outside is Religion, which consists in intercourse between man and a supernatural God: if this intercourse be impossible, then whatever delights man may find within his own nature, or whatever peace and friendship he may establish between himself and the power which shuts him off from God, he cannot have any of those comforts or aids which can properly be called religious. The power which shuts him in is physical science, which has been drawing its lines so closely round man's life that contact with what lies beyond nature seems to some no longer possible for man. We all know how long the siege has been progressing. Its commencement goes back as far in history as human thought can reach. From the very beginning it was known that man had to do not merely with God, but with nature. But the sphere in which he had to do with God seemed very large, and the restraints and difficulties which nature opposed to communication with God seemed far off and comprehended but a small portion of life. The whole world of thought, of will, and of religion was untouched by material laws and free for intercourse with God. How differently we feel now. We have seen the lines drawn closer and closer. Many parts of human action which once seemed the pure product of choice are now declared to be the undoubted result of man's physical conditions. His virtues and his vices are alike traced to material causation. The blame and the punishment which are awarded to vice and the praise which we give to virtue are proclaimed to be themselves the involuntary expression of the feelings which the acts inspire, feelings which are the result of experiences of hurt or benefit, stored up through many ages, and which are as purely physical in their origin as the acts which produce them, or as the consequences which the acts have yielded in life.

And finally, to complete the process, man's very religion itself, which he had regarded as the sure testimony of his connexion with a supernatural world, is asserted to be as physical in its origin as the rest. It is the fruit of circumstance, inevitably developed at certain stages of human life, and in certain outward conditions, and changing its form as evolution proceeds and the environments of life are altered. Its own supposition, that it deals with the supernatural, is itself accounted for by purely natural causes. It is indeed obviously open to the defenders of religion to rejoin, "If everything be due to nature, to what, or to whom, are we to ascribe the origin of nature itself?" But even if the answer to this question were given as religious men desire, it would not be enough for religion. It would not suffice for the maintenance of religion that we should recognise a connexion with God so indirect and distant as that which binds us to the unknowable source, in ages immeasurably distant, of a series of development from which by inexorable law every thing within and without us, including our religion itself, has grown. All the actual forms of our life and of our religion would in that case be traced to our material conditions, and not to the distant original impulse from which these had sprung. It would be with nature, and not with God, that our immediate dealings would be. Nature would be the Mayor of the Palace, and God the unseen and inactive King, whose only known function is to give authority to the real ruler.

49. Yet even upon the supposition that we have now no direct dealings except with nature, the appearance which supernatural belief presents of being natural to man raises an argument for a necessary belief in it on our part which it is difficult to set aside. This nature with which we have to do inexorably frames and fashions not merely our surroundings but ourselves. The very make of our own minds, and all their powers, are the result of operations of nature which we cannot resist. Every faculty of the mind, as memory, association, reasoning, is the laborious acquisition of unnumbered ages of development. We cannot alter the operation of these mental processes, and it is to no purpose for us to criticise them. It is found by experience that we may neglect to cultivate them in ourselves, and if we do we shall miss vast benefits. But the processes are what development has made them, and we must accept them as they are, or renounce them at the cost of missing our human inheritance and becoming less than men.

<small>Natural belief in the supernatural.</small>

Now among the mental processes which the countless generations of mankind in the past have acquired, practised, and bequeathed, religion holds a place, and it seems impossible to deny that religion has always included belief in the supernatural.[1] It is a very serious matter for any one in these last times to say that religion is not what the mass of mankind who have practised it have always supposed it to be. The audacity of such a contradiction of the voice of the majority is vastly increased when the person who utters it is a believer in evolution: for it means then that one who is the creation of the past, and possesses the very faculties of intellect by which his irreligious arguments are framed from the evolution of the race to which he belongs, shall refuse to receive a certain portion of what the past has bequeathed

---

[1] "He" [who desires to overthrow the faith in aught higher than nature and physical necessity] "cannot be ignorant that the vast majority of the human race in all ages and in all nations have believed to the contrary: that there is not a language on earth in which he could argue for ten minutes in support of his scheme without sliding into words and phrases that imply the contrary. It has been said that the Arabic has a thousand names for a lion; but this would be a trifle compared with the number of superfluous phrases and useless synonyms that would be found in an *index expurgatorius* of any European dictionary constructed on the principles of a consistent and strictly consequential materialism."—Coleridge, *Aids to Reflection*, vol. i. p. 101.

to him, on the ground that it does not approve itself to his reason. If evolution be true, and the whole human race be, as it teaches us, bound together by a chain that cannot be broken, what powers or faculties can one individual have thus to reject an acquisition of the whole race? The implicit obedience to nature which the doctrines of evolution impose upon every individual binds him to obey nature, even when she presses on him a belief in the supernatural as a necessary condition of his place in the system of nature. And if he should claim that it lies in his power to reject any part of his human inheritance, as, for instance, the cultivation of his memory or his social or sexual instincts, at least he must renounce all power to pick and choose out of what has been handed down to him, and pretend to accept part of religion without accepting belief in the supernatural. We must take what is given by nature and natural evolution to our minds in the form in which it is given, or not at all: and the pretence of a religion without the supernatural contradicts nature, which in every age has practised supernatural religion, and no other.

50. This seems strong. But we admit that

even this would hardly be enough for religion. The mind of a man who should try to give himself to religion because the natural development of his race has imposed it on him, while at the same time this very obedience itself is rendered on the ground that nature is his only teacher, would be in a strange, self-contradictory condition. His belief in the supernatural would be rendered only on natural grounds, and would resemble the half-hearted obedience to a usurper which the adherents of a rightful king could bring themselves to give at the bidding of their legitimate master himself. Their very service would be rendered on a principle which forbids it to gain complete possession of their deepest faith or their truest affections. And yet this perplexed state of mind seems to be the furthest point in unbelief that is possible for those who wish to give their whole belief to nature and to accept, without self-chosen and insubordinate reservations, whatever comes to them from their constitution as it is.

<small>This would not be enough for religion. But nature does not cover the whole field.</small>

But has it indeed come to this? Has nature really so closed us in that there is no direct access to God any longer possible? It is not so. There remains still a direct communication with Him open through our personality, that mysterious self which abides with us all through life and comes into action in every moment. Here lies a spot on which physical science has not planted its flag. Here is something within the bounds of nature for which nature does not account. It is an open road to the regions beyond nature. And the gap in the circle which nature draws around us is large enough to admit religion with all its ensigns and its divine Captain at its head. We may leave to science all that it has ever claimed either in our outward environment or in our inward constitution, if it will only leave to us that inner shrine of ourself which a dark veil hides even from our own understanding but which is capable of containing the presence of God, and that intercourse with personal life beyond ourselves to which we stand committed by our social instincts, and which involves all the mystery of faith in God. In God's action upon the human personality exercised directly, we might find the sphere of all those answers to our prayers and aspirations which come under the title of gifts of grace. And vast effects, even upon nature itself, might be brought about through influences directly exerted upon the spirit of man. It is hard to say what class of circumstances in the life of man would have to be excepted from the sphere of religion, even if we were to allow that the primary sphere of religion is not nature, but the personality of man. But if we believe in God as the Creator of our secret selves, with all their wonderful powers and connexions, we must needs ascribe to Him a kind of power in nature which is akin to that which our own will exercises. And religion among mankind seems to have been guided by this consciousness. Nature, indeed, speaks of God to a man who has already found God very near to him, in his mouth and in his heart. But it is extremely doubtful whether nature has ever spoken of God for the first time to a man who had never found God through his own consciousness, or through that intercourse with his fellow men which wakens him to the lessons of his own consciousness by presenting to him other beings who are partakers of his personality and helpers in its life.

51. A curious fact in the history of religion

is explained by the supposition that it is through his own consciousness and through the knowledge of other men whom an instinct of his conscious-

Man reaches God through man. ness recognises as having the same nature as himself, that man reaches God. Mr. Herbert Spencer has busied himself for a great number of years in collecting, with the aid of fellow-workers in many lands, facts bearing upon the social habits of various races. Great attention, therefore, is due to his authority when he informs us that in no case is nature-worship the earliest form of religion found among barbarous men. According to him, the worship of ancestors, the ghosts of tribal chieftains, is the earliest germ out of which advances in religion are developed.

Now this is a state of facts which seems very difficult to account for upon Mr. Spencer's own theory as to what religion is and where it finds its hold upon human nature. That theory lays down that as well in human nature as everywhere else, we have to do with an unknowable power. The first principle of agnosticism requires that the unknowable shall be recognised as underlying every part of life and nature equally; for if its influence be found more in any phenomenon or any series or combination of phenomena than in any other, this amounts to a revelation. The unknowable is then preferring certain species of phenomena, and something about its nature is thereby known. Now, if the unknowable be diffused with an absolute equality, why should barbarous mankind have agreed everywhere to find religion—which, according to Mr. Spencer, means but to recognise the unknowable—in one only species of phenomena, namely, the spirit of man? But if, as seems rather to be the case, it is not everywhere equally in nature, but specially in man himself, that man discovers the mystery which leads him to religion, it is not difficult to see why the earliest efforts after a religion in barbarous races should take the form of the worship of human spirits: or why, if we prefer so to put it, men degraded from a better knowledge of God should mark their earliest efforts after recovery or their last dim recollections of ancestral beliefs in the supernatural, with this human form.

52. The most elementary connexion which the mysterious character of our own personality has with religion is simply the negative one which

results from our sense of a dark place and a part unaccounted for found in the very centre of our own being. There is an imperative desire in our minds to account for things. And what we mean by accounting for things is tracing them to the causation of facts preceding, which according to the known connexion of series of events in the world were capable of producing them. Now, however much in our life and being we may set down as being on this principle accounted for, we are always conscious of something which is not. When we say "I did so and so," there may be a good deal, let us even say all of the thing done, which is satisfactorily accounted for by bodily constitution, acquired habits, and surrounding circumstances. But even if the whole of the act were so accounted for, this does not account for the agent who did it. That little word I, which claims the thing done, and the powers by which it was done, for its own, and yet stands separate from both, expresses an element in the action not accounted for by any precedent earthly facts. And it constantly forces itself upon our attention as finding no sufficient cause or source in any

First step from the mystery in human life to religion found in the mere sense of the mystery.

earthly circumstance. Let us compare the ease with which we trace the habits, desires, and actions of any other man or our own to circumstances which have gone before, with the difficulty, or rather impossibility, which we experience in supposing that these or any other circumstances account for the self in which these habits or acts are inherent.[1] We say, He is hungry, or, He is drunken—and we readily ascribe the hunger or the drunkenness to the circumstances which are known to be capable of producing such a state. And if we want to trace it further back we find adequate causes for it in the physiological facts of man's frame and in the history of his evolution. But it is in vain that we attempt to restrict the meaning of the word "he" to anything which can be ascribed to these material circumstances. There is always something more in it than that which may be traced to such a source. And the recognition of this mysterious fact is not an effort of thought which a few can

---

[1] "La personne n'est pas l'individu. L'individu se compose de tous les accidents particuliers qui distinguent un homme d'un autre : ces accidents perissent avec nous : c'est la chair. La personne est la conscience de l'impersonnel : c'est l'esprit."—Janet, *La Morale*, preface.

reach, but lies upon the surface and is felt always and by everybody, and most of all by men in respect to themselves. This unaccountable consciousness accompanies us through life and lies at the root of life. It must have been felt by the lowest savage who ever had a human consciousness, and it remains equally mysterious within the being of the most accomplished man of science.

53. Now this must always impart a mysterious character to human life. It is impossible for men to maintain the self-satisfied sense of knowing all about themselves except by excluding from their minds a fact which ought to lie nearer to them than any other, since it lies at the beginning of all action and of all thought. And this fact is, that while they may know all about the surroundings of the self, the self they cannot know. Even if we could know to the very last all the powers and all the laws of our body and of our mind, that would only bring into greater prominence the humbling but certain truth that we do not know how we came to be ourselves, or in what ourselves consist.

<small>This even alone would be a religion.</small>

If we could imagine this ignorance about our own being felt by a perfectly self-restrained mind determined not to travel out of logical convictions, it might still be capable in itself of yielding something not unworthy of the name of a religion. This special mystery in ourselves would not be the impotent thing for moral and religious purposes which the general admission of an unknowable element in all things undoubtedly is. An unknowable equally diffused every where is not the concern of any creature in particular. It affords the most striking example possible of the truth that what is everybody's business is nobody's business. But to find a mysterious element in ourselves which does not, so far as we know, present itself in the same form in any other creature, animate or inanimate, is a special call upon us. It cannot but impart a feeling of awe to our self-consciousness. It cannot but keep us waiting anxiously to know whether perhaps from that dark abyss out of which we spring and from which our personal life is continually issuing, something may not come in the present state or in some future one to guide us amidst the difficulties of our life, and to furnish us with some clue to its perplexities.

54. But we could not expect that the mass of minds to which the mystery of being has been brought home would treat it with such self-restraint as to abstain in default of better knowledge from filling the void with imaginations. That the imaginations of heathen faiths have their origin not so much in the general mystery of nature as in the special mystery of human nature is testified by the human character which all religions bear. Whether the processes of nature have any such share at all in the origin of mythologies as a well-known school ascribes to them may be well doubted, and has been doubted by some who have the best right to speak. But even if we were to ascribe this prominent and originating place in the history of religion to the awe and wonder with which men viewed the processes of nature, the fact that these natural processes appear everywhere symbolised and embodied in stories of human life shows the more strongly that for man the mystery of nature is concentrated in the mystery of man. Buddhism, that strange religion, seems

But human nature fills the void with imaginations.

above all others to feel the burden and the pain of our existence as separate selves and teaches the final absorption and loss of personality in the ocean of being or not being. But Buddhism even by its opposition to personality, and its strain and struggle with the fact of this awful gift, and its very desire after impersonal existence, testifies to the fact that personality is the great thought which occupies its attention and furnishes its motive. And as a religion actually existing and practised by men, Buddhism loses all its strained longing after the loss of personality, and becomes just as human and just as fully embodied in the belief and worship of a person as any form of paganism.

In most religions, however degraded be their popular form, there is discoverable an original germ of purer and more spiritual character. Behind the sensuous forms of the popular deities the one spiritual source of all lies hid, unknown to the multitude, but still confessed in ancient books or rites that have lost their spiritual meaning to those who practise them. But although the one spiritual deity be free from the bodily form and from the sensual associations of the popular divinities, there is no reason for imagining that He is less truly personal. In retreating from sensuous into spiritual conceptions of God, we are not retreating from the personal into the impersonal, but from material associations into true personality. We are seeking an author and source of our own essential life. So argues St. Paul: "God that made the world and all things therein dwelleth not in temples made with hands, neither is worshipped with men's hands, as though He needed anything, seeing He giveth unto all life and breath and all things." And the process of degradation which takes place when a spiritual conception of deity becomes embodied in earthly forms, and then debased by superstition and sensuality, finds not only its counterpart but its close companion in the degradation of the human personality itself, imprisoned, it knows not how, in a human body, and forced to acknowledge as its own an earthly sensual life which is wholly beneath it.

55. We have been regarding our self merely as a dark and unexplained part of our constitution. That is one element in our conception of it. But this confession of our ignorance as to what we

are and how we came to be is not the whole of our conception of self, nor is this ignorance the only part of our idea of personality in which religion finds a place of lodgment. For our self, though incomprehensible in its nature, is revealed in action. It is not a negation. It is indeed the source of all activity, and though mysterious in its being is yet in its work the best known of all agencies which we find to exist. It is the cause of all action and of everything that results from action. It is impossible for us to refrain from tracing events to their causes, and there are multitudes of events which, traced up to their causes, bring us at last to ourselves. We caused them: which means, not that this or that faculty which we possess was their cause, but that the mystery behind the faculty, which obliges us to call it our own, moved the faculty and caused the result. It is true that many collateral causes may be named as accounting for the form which our actions took: but all these would have been nothing, or at least nothing to us, unless we ourselves had supplied the spark which set the whole machinery at work.

The second step is found in the necessity of connecting the mysterious self in its active character with some power and cause beyond.

Now is this cause of all that we are or do to be regarded as itself uncaused? The word cause is here used in its ordinary sense of an adequate antecedent, the sense in which we every moment demand to know the cause of everything that happens and anything that exists, or at least suppose that there is a cause of everything, whether we know that cause or not. Our bodies are built up and constituted by a series of natural events, and every position of every particle has its natural cause. Though natural causation be not so clear in respect of our intellectual and emotional faculties, yet we see that natural causation rules them in part, and we know not but that it may rule them altogether. Our powers of mind, our passions, and our preferences are caused, we know not how far, by facts preceding. But as to that self which lies behind body and mind, passions and preferences, we cannot say the same. The derivation of all, both of our bodily and mental powers, from previous facts in the world's progress, does not trace the origin of the self to the same source. Far from it. The more completely and absolutely we give up the whole series of bodily and mental action with all the powers from which it proceeds, to the examination of science, and the more willingly we accept the natural causation which science has found for some of them, acknowledging that some day a similar causation will be found for all: by so much the more clearly do we see that no natural antecedent has been found for the personal ingredient in the series which claims the beginning of all for its own and mingles strangely with the whole. We ourselves are neither our bodies nor yet our minds: it is a necessity of thought to distinguish ourselves from both.

56. Does then human personality alone among all the powers that are at work in the world hang in the air? Is the cord on which our whole life depends itself attached to nothing? Does no antecedent fact, no being or existence anywhere, account for this personality in the sense of preceding and producing it by some appropriate bond of connexion? It is quite impossible for us to think so. Our personality demands an adequate and appropriate, that is to say, a personal cause. One would think that this is obvious enough to be understood and felt by every one. The notion

Impossibility of regarding it as uncaused.

of a great First Cause, well founded though it be, yet may lie too far back to have influenced universal mankind. But the existence of a personal being, a Being above us, to whom our personality attaches itself, and from whom it proceeds, has been proved by experience to lie close to the minds and hearts of all men. We feel after Him and strive to find Him, although He be not far from every one of us, for in Him we live and move and have our being—as a poet even of the heathen themselves has said, "For we are also His offspring." The apostle's appeal is made to the consciousness of his Athenian audience and to the testimony borne to that consciousness by those who in past ages gave a voice to the general mind. And it is surely well founded.

57. Nevertheless this appeal is disregarded by one of the popular systems of the day. The Philosophy of the Unconscious finds, as its name denotes, its very essence in the belief that we are not of the race of God in the sense which the apostle claims, and do not find Him near us in that human consciousness which sets us apart from nature. In the philosophy of the unconscious,

A personal cause required with which to connect our human personality. The Philosophy of the Unconscious.

God is found in nature as the cause, but when we come to man and to that conscious life which makes man what he is God is the cause no longer. Von Hartmann traces the marks of design in nature, and in man considered as a part of nature, with a clearness and power equal to that of Paley and a wealth of knowledge far above him. In every quarter we are bidden to discern the existence of some phenomenon which could not have come by chance as the sufficient proof of the existence of an intellect and a power adequate to cause it. The arrangement is everywhere considered to prove that the thought and conception of the arrangement must have previously existed, and have been aimed at as an end by that incomprehensible power which works in nature. But when after pursuing this process through nature and through all the unconscious part of man's frame we come at last to that highest part of man, his consciousness of himself as a personal existence, there we are bidden to stop. We are no longer to argue that this wonderful fact is a proof that the thought and conception of it existed beforehand in the mind of that power by which it has been produced; but Consciousness has been originated by a Being which is itself unconscious.

Man's soul stands in a very strange position in this philosophy.[1] It is something which comes as illegitimate children come into the world, unexpected and unprovided for, and very unwelcome. Everything else in nature proceeds systematically from adequate causes, that is to say, from causes which implicitly conceive and intend their effects: but not so the soul and the consciousness of man. To allow that this was conceived or intended beforehand would be to ascribe consciousness to the all-producing power: for how could consciousness be intended or aimed at except by a conscious being? And to recognise a conscious origin of all things would be to acknowledge God: the All One in this case is no longer the unconscious. The consciousness of man, alone among phenomena, must not be regarded as an intended end. This is an inconsistent position. It is to stop short in an unwarranted and unreasonable manner in the application of a method of reasoning which has been used with effect through every part of nature and being. To

[1] *Philosophy of the Unconscious*, vol. ii. p. 248. (Eng. trans.).

be consistent you must either recognise consciousness both in the divine cause and in the human effect, or if you deny it in the cause you must deny it in the effect, and pronounce that what seems consciousness in man is not a true fact at all, but an unreal imagination.

There can be no doubt at all that the sense of a mystery in our nature, and the necessity of connecting our personality with an adequate cause preceding, have been widely operative among mankind. Some trouble indeed is required to reflect upon these mental operations, as upon any others; those which are most instinctive and most common are often the most difficult to analyse by reflection. And these mental wants may take a form in highly cultivated minds of which those which are in a lower place of the scale are quite incapable. The developed intellect separates the mystery of human nature from all the other mysteries of creation, and realises it in its own distinctness: and demands a cause so far back as in the beginning of all things and which finds no external cause of its own existence. These refinements may be unthought of by uncivilised men, and perhaps even by the mass of the civilised to this day. But the dim feeling of something wonderful and something above nature in the personality of man, and the instinct which prevents man from believing that his inmost nature attaches itself to nothing as its cause, are feelings not beyond the most undeveloped minds that can be called human. They are not more wonderful than the other mental processes which savages and children admittedly use. And as matter of fact, we know that no race of mankind has been so entirely bound down by habit to a sensual existence as not to have made efforts after expressing its sense of the mystery of personal life and finding a cause why man is man.

58. Even speculative interest in the question alone might suffice to drive men to a religion. The curious intellect asserts its claims and demands its employment among all mankind, and the imagination helps to supply what the curious intellect seeks. But there is another power in human nature which removes the question whether a divine source lies behind our human personality out of the sphere of speculation and invests it at once with the most practical character. This part

Third step. The moral nature of man imparts a practical character to the demand of a cause of personality.

of human nature, though like many others liable to be obscured in this or that individual, and to be overborne by passions and interests for a time, is yet indeed as essential a component of man's constitution as any faculty, and holds not only a place, but a commanding place, among the ruling principles of his life. It is conscience, which lives in human nature like a rightful king whose claim can never be forgotten by his people even though they dethrone and misuse him, and whose presence on the seat of judgment can alone make the nation to be at peace within itself.

It is very well known that of late years many attempts have been made not merely to subject the history of conscience to scientific examination —a claim which every principle and every belief must contentedly submit to—but actually to prove that the formation of conscience is due to natural evolution. When such a theory is held in its complete and only consistent form, it means that the natural pleasures of the senses are the basis upon which all choice of action on the part of man must originally rest. Such pleasures are so very often at the disposal of others to give, that the approval of us on the part of others which may

M

lead them to give us pleasures comes through association to be valued as a good in itself. Now communities are naturally led to confer their approval upon those who show themselves willing to be of service to the common welfare; and as the pleasurable actions which are serviceable to the community are sufficiently rewarded by being pleasurable, the community reserves its chief praise for those actions which require large compensations to induce any one to do them, that is to say, such as are self-denying. The families in which self-denial becomes an inheritance are kept from extinction by the help of the races to which they belong, while the selfish are permitted to die away, or are deliberately destroyed because of use to nobody. And the races in which self-sacrifice for the sake of the community or the practice of those virtues which experience proves beneficial to it most widely prevails are naturally those which maintain themselves in the struggle for existence. Thus self-denial and virtue grow more and more to be inherited attributes of human nature, and subjects of preference in themselves, until at last we recognise in the determination of a saint to endure martyrdom rather than deny his convictions, a transmuted form of the same desire for pleasure which in a remote age led his ancestors to gratify passion without regard for the consequences to others or even to themselves.[1]

59. It seems pretty obvious that this view of the nature of conscience if it were ever generally recognised in a community would stop moral growth. It might have a certain tendency to make people practise the self-denying duties (if such they could be called) which had actually by the development of ages preceding become

The purely natural theory of the growth of conscience is morally fatal and intellectually inadequate.

[1] See George Eliot's statement of her moral system in the "Notes on the Spanish Gipsy" (*Life of George Eliot*, chapter xv.). "Love, pity, constituting sympathy and generous joy with regard to the lot of our fellow men, comes in—has been growing since the beginning—enormously enhanced by wider vision of results—by an imagination actively interested in the lot of mankind generally: and these feelings become piety—*i.e.* loving, willing, submissive and heroic Promethean effort towards high possibilities which may result from our individual life. There is really no moral 'sanction' but this inward impulse. The will of God is the same thing as the will of other men compelling us to work, and avoid what they have seen to be harmful to social existence. Disjoined from any perceived good, the divine will is simply so much as we have ascertained of the facts of existence which compel obedience at our peril." It is the result of this theory that the author's works, nobly as they depict the moral struggles of those who have a noble ideal, are neither fitted to enforce a noble ideal on those who have it not, nor yet to raise the moral ideal of mankind beyond the standard which has actually been reached by the race. To do these things has been the task of writers and workers inspired from a higher source than the actual attainments of the human society.

pleasurable to them. It would enable men to see that the greatest happiness for self may often be found in apparent self-sacrifice. But the same knowledge that pleasure is the first principle of morality, which thus stamps our actual attainments in morality as so many pleasures which have become necessary to our highest enjoyment, will forbid us to go at all beyond the amount of self-denial which can be felt to have become pleasurable. Every principle of nature will forbid a man to extend the area of his self-sacrifice, and will bid him keep the few self-regarding pleasures that are left him. Conscience will be regarded as an inmate of the garrison whose connexions with the enemies of our comfort outside are extremely suspicious. It will be constantly accused of wanting to lead us into degrees of virtue up to which we are not educated and which are not for our happiness. It cannot be expelled, and indeed wise lovers of themselves could not wish to expel a faculty which may yield pleasure so exquisite. But it must be carefully confined within the space to which it can prove its title; and it must be kept under strict watch and control. And the growth of conscience would thus be stopped even if we could suppose that its present height of attainment would continue unimpaired.

We cannot avoid recognising such a tendency in these physical and natural theories of the origin of conscience: and it affords a sound argument against maintaining the theories. Some people assume, without much consideration, that it is always best that the truth should be known. But if it were true that conscience rests only on a natural basis, and that the call to practise virtue if our nature has been so developed as to be adapted to virtue, is precisely of the same character as the call to practise vice if it be vice for which we are naturally fitted, it would seem to be expedient that this false truth should be concealed from the mass of mankind. But, moral reasons apart, it is most unlikely, as matter of bare theory, that an account of conscience of this character can be complete. It does not account for the facts. It may indeed account for a great deal of the form and mould of moral action, and the particular conduct which morality demands from age to age. But it does not account for the fiery power which drives the molten metal all glowing to fill the form. It does not account for the spirit of growth and the steady longing for greater strength and wider application than it already possesses, which is even a more characteristic attribute of conscience than its level working within the sphere of duty which has been cleared for it. It does not explain the mystical element in conscience; the readiness which it has always shown to ally itself with religion and which is observable even in cases where all fixed belief has been entirely cast away. Nor does the natural theory account for the intensely personal character of conscience. It makes the growth of morality resemble that of a plant, as if personality were passive in the process, and found itself changed from sensuality to self-sacrifice as a river finds its colour changed from gray to blue by simply passing from beneath the cloud to beneath the sky. No doubt a great deal in our life, and even in our moral life, is of this passive character. But how apathetically do we regard such passive habits! How little do we ascribe them to ourselves! How little do we trouble our conscience about actions, good or bad, which are really imposed on us by our constitution and our circumstances! When conscience comes into play it makes the most imperious distinctions between our self and our circumstances, habits, and propensities, mental or bodily. It says to us that we must not hand over the blame or the responsibility to our outward circumstances, nor to our bodily necessities, nor yet to our mental habits, whether inherited or acquired. It is not any of these, but you yourself that are responsible ; so speaks conscience.[1] Very often we pretend to think this personal treatment on the part of our conscience unreasonable. We follow circumstances, or desire, or habit. We live that impersonal life of a thing, carried about by divers currents, which, from the point of view of physical science, would really seem to be our only true life. But it does not answer. When conscience awakes nothing seems real and nothing true except that personal

---

[1] Compare St. Augustine's description of his unawakened condition (*Confess.* v. 10) : "Adhuc enim mihi videbatur non esse nos qui peccamus sed nescio quam aliam in nobis peccare naturam: et delectabat superbiam meam extra culpam esse : et cum aliquid mali fecissem non confiteri me fecisse ut sanares animam meam quoniam peccabat tibi sed excusare eam amabam et accusare nescio quid aliud quod mecum esset et ego non essem." And the reverse in his converted state (*Confess.* viii. 10): "Ego cum deliberabam ut jam servirem Domino Deo meo sicut diu disposueram, ego eram qui volebam, ego qui nolebam : ego, ego eram."

On the other hand Montaigne : "Those passions which only touch the outward part of us cannot be said to be ours. To make them so there must be a concurrence of the whole man."

life which regards all things, both without the mind and within it, as the instruments with which it has to work. The nature of the instrument will, to be sure, greatly determine the results of the work. But the responsibility rests on the workman who employs them.

60. There is no word better than the word responsibility to express the feeling which the exercise of conscience draws out in us. And the word responsibility clearly implies a superior power behind conscience. All men feel that conscience makes them responsible. To whom responsible? An awful question. Is it to society? Society has no claim to exercise such a judgment. It has no such rights over us, has conferred no such benefits upon us, has no such accurate knowledge of what we have done compared with what we could do, as might fit it to receive or deliver an account. But above all, society is not the author or giver of that personal existence and power in which the very character of conscience lies. Is it, then, to ourselves that we are responsible? The words express a great truth. But if we are to consider them sufficient to explain the whole nature of

Conscience tells us we are responsible. To whom?

conscience, we must take ourselves as including something more than the powers of our minds as we can understand them. The self to which conscience is responsible is more than the mere individual. It speaks not in the name of the individual alone; it is self, but more than self. We feel that we are put in charge of ourselves by a higher power and a higher right, and conscience never speaks without implicitly reminding us of this commission which it holds from a mysterious authority beyond our life. That we feel there is a tribunal beyond ourselves is plainly proved by the apprehension of punishment which conscience uniformly displays when wrong has been done. The punishment apprehended may clothe itself for the imagination in various forms. It may consist in bodily tortures feared in the next world; it may be temporal chastisements in this life; it may be of a more spiritual character, and consist in afflictions of soul or the sense of divine disapproval, whether here or hereafter. But one of these as much as the other is punishment, and implies a superhuman power which inflicts the penalty. We can see in the very nature of conscience itself that mystical element which explains the close alliance between it and religion, to which history uniformly testifies. Upon any theory of morality which is capable of engendering life or enthusiasm there must be the recognition of a moral ideal floating before the mind. It must be a standard higher than anything which the life has yet realised, something which has never presented itself to the senses or the intellect. Yet, though it be an ideal, it must possess such reality that we feel it would be death to miss it. And it is futile to doubt the assistance which is imparted to morality when this ideal is invested with the truth which religion gives to it, and conscience sees itself embodied in a divine being, the fountain of all morality.

61. This in the sphere of morals is the very same demand which the sense of our own personality makes in the sphere of thought and existence. The consciousness of our own personality demands that we trace it up to a cause and find the source of ourselves in a personal being above us. And the nature of conscience demands that we trace up its warnings and its work to a cause, and regard it as the voice of a

Our personality demands a personal God, our moral nature a moral God.

moral being above us. The closest connexion exists between these two analogies. The relationship of the terms consciousness and conscience, which are in fact but forms of the same word, testifies to the fact that it is in the action of conscience that man's consciousness of himself is chiefly experienced. His consciousness might remain apathetic and lifeless enough; it might never lead him up to its divine source, or if it did, that God to whom it led him might be a mere stranger uninterested in him and uninteresting to him, if it were not that conscience presses it on him as matter of awful importance that he should guide his personal life so as to obtain the approval of this higher personality in whom it has its origin. But we want not only God's approval but God's help. And He reveals Himself to us as not only the source of the personal life of which we are conscious and of the character and aim of personal life which is revealed to us in conscience, but also as the abiding source of life and activity both in consciousness and in conscience. He has in Himself the life which He gives to ourselves. And as our conscience bids ourselves to live, but not to live for self, we recognise in God self-existence, but not existence for self alone. He bids us love and must be love Himself. And in Him our personality finds its freedom from slavery to the natural world and its true character of complete self-assertion mixed with complete self-abnegation. I live, yet not I, but Christ liveth in me.

V.

WE KNOW GOD IN NATURE AND MAN.

"And God said, Let us make man in our image, after our likeness: and let them have dominion over the fish of the sea, and over the fowl of the air, and over the cattle, and over all the earth."—GEN. i. 26.

62. WHATEVER has been urged in the preceding pages has depended upon one principle: that in man's self, and in the essential part of self which constitutes man a person, there is a mystery. There is a fact, a reality, a power, which cannot be explained to the mind. It cannot be connected with anything in nature, nor can it be shown capable of arising through natural causes; yet its existence cannot be ignored by any one who lives. *Recapitulation.*

The belief that our personality is not comprehensible to us as part of the system of nature does not at all imply any attempt to except man, or any part of man's constitution, from the range of natural science. On the contrary, the whole force of the argument depends upon the fearless application of the methods of natural science to every part of man's bodily and mental life. For after we have discovered how complete is the dominion of physical causation in both the body and mind of man; when the line of material connexion recognised in the inanimate world and in the lower creation has been also proved to include man's nervous system, and to make his feelings and acts as truly links in the chain as are the winds and the tides; when motives and impressions of the mind are found to be the counterpart and accompaniment in the mental sphere of material contact in the bodily, and to follow their own laws of causation just as inexorably and as regularly as motion follows upon impulse in the world of matter—then these acknowledged principles and the unrestricted application which we make of them bring into its true prominence the fact that they do not account for all. If there were any parts of the body or mind of man to which we refused to apply the laws of matter and motion and the corresponding laws of mental motive there would be little mystery about the affair. Here would be a definite part of the world either of thought or of matter, within which we should know the secret to be hid. As of the source of some great river, we should know, if not where and what it is, at least within what limits it must lie.

But now the whole region has been searched through, and the source cannot be discovered. We find the river running at the furthest point to which we can reach. No anatomy either of the body or of the mind, though practised without any restraint upon the whole of human nature, has made any advance towards showing us how or whence the sense of personality and the indelible conviction of the freedom of the will come to us. We cannot understand how man, if he were indeed a mere link in the chain of physical causes, should possess such a sense. And even though we were to believe that to some higher intelligence, nature with its law, and personality with its freedom, might fall into one system, that does not make it possible for us to unite them. We are what we are, and have no faculties but our own wherewith to discern truth and reality. For us it is as impossible to unite as it is impossible to disengage the bodily and material from the spiritual. But though personality or will in itself cannot be discovered, yet the effects of it and man's conviction that he possesses it are to be seen wherever he lives or works. Neither man nor man's world would be what they are if his personality and his free will were not parts of his consciousness, of which it is impossible for him to divest himself for a moment. His intercourse with his fellow men would be something of a wholly different character from what it is if he had not the conviction that they too are persons. He cannot prove it of them; he cannot see it in them. But when he behaves to them as if they were persons, he finds everything fit the presumption, and if he behaves to them as if they were not, all his own life and all theirs become degraded.

We have seen that the mystery of human life and human intercourse has always led men to religion. The very knowledge that there is something in our being which must ever remain mysterious to us is in itself a kind of religion; but much more when we consider that this mysterious part of our nature is that which is the source of all personal life and action in us; and that along with personal life and action there comes to us an imperious direction to make life and action moral. These are the experiences of every one. And they are inexplicable except on the supposition of a divine agent who makes us what we are and requires of us what we ought to do.

63. Now in speaking thus we have been regarding the personality of man and his moral powers as powers and forces separate from nature, and capable of being entirely distinguished from everything in nature. And this they certainly are and have ever been felt to be. Although self and the will by which self acts are mysteries, that does not in the least imply that there is any doubt about the existence of self. We know not what it is in itself, but we know that it is. It has a separate existence of its own so far as anything can be said to have a separate existence: and this is a necessary qualification, for nothing can be conceived as existing in absolute separation from other things. We cannot name anything or even conceive it without thereby distinguishing it from other things and

Fourth step. Man must be regarded not only in his separation from nature, but in his connexion with nature;

implying its relation to them; its existence implies theirs. But the relation of self to nature is one of distinction and of opposition.

Yet we cannot make the slightest attempt at grasping the notion of this central person and will of man without thinking of it as working upon nature and matter. The self-consciousness of man is that which enables him to think of himself; but he cannot think without employing both mental and physical powers which are part of the system of nature. It is the will of man which enables him to act. But he cannot act without putting himself into relations with the material world, even from the very earliest moment of the action which observation or thought can trace. These are the strange and wonderful conditions under which self exists and works.

We find ourselves obliged to attribute to our personal self a kind of originating or creative power. In every moment of life and action, and in every operation of the will, there is to our consciousness a kind of new beginning of life unfettered and unattached to anything that has gone before. It is true that when we inquire and reflect, we find that as the matter presents itself to thought, this is not at all the case, but that everything we desire and everything we do seems bound by the strictest ties of causation to the external course of things, and could not be what it is if they were in any wise different. But this conclusion is the result of reflection and inquiry; it passes as a theory into our minds, but it does not form part of the consciousness which we use in action and in life. For these, life is taken up anew at every moment; the will has the initiative, and an act of will is the very first step in every act of life. But the will cannot take one step forward, no, not so much as to make its own existence perceived, without finding itself involved with the world. The world is its necessary instrument.

The world is not a tractable instrument, and the relations in which the will stands to it are distant if not of an unfriendly character. The world has its own laws and it entirely declines to be made the instrument of the will, except on the condition that its laws are to be strictly obeyed. It yields itself to man's use only with absolute reservation of all its own rights, and it never forgets even one moment to assert them;

so that when an action is analysed in which human will has come into play, it is entirely impossible to separate the elements of will and of natural law from each other, and say that so much was due to the will and so much to the law. The will and the law work together, inextricably bound to one another all through the action.

This is the condition of human life: so we must think in order to live. If we were to surrender the notion that we possess wills capable of influencing the world, our life would come to a standstill. We should wait for nature to move us instead of taking the initiative ourselves. But we are widely mistaken if we dream of the possibility of making even the very slightest movement towards any work, not to say of carrying any work into effect, without so exactly submitting to the laws of nature that everything we do shall be capable of being described as their work. And this we cannot understand. Besides the original impossibility of comprehending what these selves of which we have so intimate a consciousness are in themselves, and how they come to exist, there is also another difficulty amounting to an impossibility in comprehending why they connect themselves with the world of matter and the laws of nature, and whence arises this extraordinary relation of mingled mastery and slavery, or rather complete mastery combined with complete slavery and how it is to be described.

64. When we find ourselves obliged to seek an antecedent cause for our personality and our will we cannot satisfy the conditions of the problem by believing in an incomprehensible Being, a mystery in Himself, corresponding to that mysterious self within us of which He is the source. *And this connexion demands a cause. Man in nature must represent God in nature.* For it belongs to the very nature of this self within us, that incomprehensible as it is in itself it is capable of placing itself in relations to nature and the laws of nature, and proving its existence and its power without any infringement of them. We shall not have found a true cause of our personality unless we have found a cause capable of accounting for this essential character of it, that in some fashion as mysterious as its own being it is capable of existing and of acting in a world the laws of which seem to leave no room for either its existence or its action.

The operations of the human will in the world have very often been used as an illustration or parallel for those of the will of God. When men have argued against the possibility of miracle on the ground of the uniformity of natural laws, it has been replied that the uniformity of natural laws does not prevent the human will from making many changes in the world and causing circumstances to happen which the laws of nature could never have brought about if will had not intervened: while all this is done without infringement of the laws of nature. Why, it is argued, should not the same on a larger and more striking scale be possible to the will of God? And if this be possible to the will of God, shall we not have miracles—not indeed in that sense which some wrongly attach to the word miracle, of infringements of the laws of nature, but in the truer sense of facts brought about in the world by such uses of natural laws as are perfectly in accordance with absolute maintenance of them, but yet would never have been made if will had not interposed to guide and direct the operations of nature?

But what is now insisted on is not the parallel

which lies between the will of man as influencing nature consistently with her laws and the will of God as doing the same; but the connexion of effect and cause which exists between these two powers. The mysterious and inscrutable personality of man, a product which no force discernible in nature alone could have yielded, leads us to a cause beyond nature. The power which this mysterious human will possesses to connect itself with nature and to work upon nature demands to be accounted for also, and mankind have found the account of the matter in believing that man with his personal will and his power of work in the world finds his origin and cause in a divine power, mysterious and supernatural, like the personality of man, but capable also like it of connexion with nature. The will of man moulding nature in conformity to natural law gives us a kind of model in miniature of that divine power in which the whole wonderful system originates.

Beyond a doubt this view of things has been very operative in leading the mind of man to God. It has operated not merely in the form of argument, but far more widely in the form of feeling, and has led mankind to believe in a Being above them, who has given them their powers to contend with nature, and has imposed the contest upon them because this contest in its human form resembles and reproduces the relations which He Himself holds to nature. Sometimes, as in the heathen religions, the subjection of man to nature is scarcely more complete or more degrading than that under which the gods also lie. Sometimes, as in the Jewish and Christian systems, the relations of God to nature lose everything of degradation, and become the instruments of the loftiest command and the most triumphant victory. Yet in both cases, and in the latter not less than the former, we have in the respective positions of God and the world a kind of picture upon a vaster scale of those which man in himself experiences. We have a transcendental and mysterious personality and a will essentially free, in inscrutable connexion with a world of matter which has laws of its own. And this will, whatever be the degree of its power over matter, never can have any power over it which is perfect or infinite: for it must ever be limited by the conditions of the material with which it deals.

65. This way of thinking about God, however it be sanctioned by the authority of mankind in general, is yet subject to an imputation considered very formidable in modern philosophy: that of anthropomorphism. We are told that to make the human will in its relations to nature the model of our conceptions of God may indeed be natural enough, but is a primitive and a savage belief which must give way as larger and more scientific ideas prevail. However, it does not appear that man and his relations to nature are, in the higher forms of this faith, made any otherwise the model of those which are ascribed to God, than as every effect must give us a kind of model of the cause to which we attribute it. Although an effect may be unlike its cause in a thousand ways, yet there must be so much resemblance that the cause shall contain in itself the capacity for producing an effect of this kind. Men have therefore found it impossible to conceive how a God entirely separate from nature, untouched and uninfluenced by any natural conditions, should have given existence to such beings as they find themselves to be, beings whose very essence consists in this, that they have an unknowable

Is this anthropomorphism?

personality inextricably united with the world of things known. Further than this, religion does not pretend to assimilate God to man. Whatever tendencies of this kind the grosser forms of religion evince have been purged away in the purer; and we find the prophetic spokesmen, both of Judaism and Christianity, exhausting the resources of language in order to express their sense of the height at which God stands above man, and the essential difference which exists between the two. It is acknowledged that all those human expressions which we are forced to make use of in reference to the nature of God must be extremely inadequate. Intellect, Personality, Will, not to speak of such terms as the hand or the eye of God, must always fall short. They are mere adaptations to human modes of thought, the necessary language in which man must be addressed. But it must be right in some sense, higher than we can understand, to apply these terms to God: else how could He have been the cause of the similar powers which they denote in us?

Of all the marks of will and design in the world the highest is the existence of minds and wills which, like those of men, are themselves capable of design. No machinery so imperatively requires us to recognise the work of a machinist as the machinery which is self-acting. When we find in nature the most wonderful adaptations of means to ends, we find ourselves forced by a mental necessity to believe in some power which has known the problem and dealt with it. We see in all such natural results a guide to the nature of their cause. For instance, in Paley's celebrated illustration, the watch is so far a guide to our conception of the watchmaker that we must believe in a watchmaker who had the idea of the watch and understood the materials of which it was to be made, and how to deal with them for the purpose in view. Where the subjects in which the design is traced are themselves unconscious it may perhaps be possible to ascribe their existence to unconscious agency. But how can unconscious agency produce conscious minds and wills? How could a power itself absolutely separate from nature, deal with the problem how to construct personalities to rule in nature and be ruled by it?

It will be found that no attempts to trace conscious personality to an unconscious cause can ever be successful. If indeed personality and consciousness in man be denied; if it be asserted that whatever man may think, he has no personality, but is only a part of nature, and that his consciousness is not what it seems but a mere unessential addition to life, having no influence or power over the real work of living; then we are able to conceive man coming from an unconscious cause, for he is in that case to all real intents and purposes unconscious himself. But this is not the position which is taken against the personality of God. It is acknowledged that consciousness and the idea of the self possess reality as a description of man's nature; but it is denied that we can ascribe them to God. If not, whence came they to man? A question which universal mankind have found it impossible to answer without bringing God and nature into conscious combination in the making of man as the soul and nature are consciously combined in man's frame and constitution.

Does it lead us to a God who is limited by nature?

66. There is an objection from quite a different quarter to which this conception of God is subject. If we make the human will in its relations to nature

the model of our ideas of God and His work in nature, how are we to defend ourselves against the charge of setting limits to the power and goodness of God? Are we not proclaiming a God of finite attributes who reflects that inability to deal with matter and the world under which man groans? The condition of the human will in relation to nature is this, that it has a wonderful independence of nature; that it has a power of command in nature which sets it above all mere natural forces; that it makes new beginnings in nature and sets agencies at work which but for it would have lain dormant, but that all the time nature has its own sphere and its own powers, and offers to the human will an instrument whose conditions must be submitted to and obeyed.

Now, when we seek behind this wonderful system of things for a cause fitted to produce it, we are led to a personality, spiritual and separate from nature; like the personality of man so far as to be its cause, and as far raised above it as the originating cause must be above any effect which flows from it. This divine source of our personality must have in perfection all that we possess imperfectly. It must, therefore, have in an original and creative sense that relation to nature which is so essential a part of our being. That initiative, that power of setting nature in motion, and determining what law shall prevail and what law shall yield, which even we in our small sphere can claim, our Maker must have in a degree infinitely higher. We have a command over natural laws which enables us to influence and direct one or two of them, while the rest of the mighty whole calmly take their way without our interference and even without our knowledge. But in Him to whom we can look as the cause of all the personalities of all mankind and of the nature with which they stand connected, this relation to natural laws must be such as to enable Him to grasp the whole system in perfect knowledge and to influence it when and as He will. Even in our little life the will holds a position of superiority to nature. It sets at work agencies which but for it never would have operated. But in the Cause of all, this must pass into such an absolute primary relation to nature, that her laws issue from Him as from their first origin.

Yet even when we have carried our faith so far

as to ascribe to God the creation of the laws of nature, and to say that while we set a few of them in motion they all have their origin in Him, must we not ascribe to nature when once at work a certain independence of God? If His perfection is to consist in His possession to a perfect degree of that independence of nature in which we recognise our own personality, the same analogy demands that nature shall be independent of Him. For us the two things go together. Man's independence of nature implies nature's independence of man. We cannot separate the will of man from nature for the purpose of exalting him, and then proceed to identify nature with the will of man for the sake of humbling her. The separation if it exists at all must be reciprocal. And it seems that the same reasoning must needs apply to God. Nature must be regarded as something objective to God, even as she is to us. And God's power in nature, however high above ours, yet must be thought of as limited and conditioned, like ours, by the conditions of the instruments with which He has to work.

And yet it is not possible to deny that such an admission is of necessity destructive of the attempt to ascribe to God an absolute omnipotence in nature. But do we, therefore, recognise only a God such as Stuart Mill was ready to believe in; a being of great though still imperfect power and goodness? That is a theory which is quite easily stated and has no element of mystery in it whatever; but it is not the faith to which we are led in seeking a source of our own personality in its combination with nature. It was natural that Stuart Mill should state the matter so, for he did not believe in human free will. But to one who apprehends the mystery of man's self as ruling nature and being ruled by it, a more mysterious deity is necessary. For there must, in the first place, be a Father of spirits, a source of the free unfettered will and of the incomprehensible self which we have within us; and this God cannot be subject to conditions or limitations. And next there must be a God of nature who must by that very fact be subject to limits in His action. We cannot wonder that the Gnostic sects of old separated these two beings; for indeed the idea of Deity is very different in each. But if we separate the God of spirits from the God of nature we have found no solution for the mystery of man's constitution, in which free will and natural law stand in real though mysterious combination. God must, therefore, be both transcendental and immanent; both beyond nature and within it.

67. We cannot expect that God's being should be divested of mystery for us when our own is so full of it. And the mystery of it consists in this, that we must ascribe perfect freedom to the God of our spirits; and perfect freedom can be nothing else but omnipotence, since freedom is plainly imperfect wherever there is anything which cannot be done. While again, we must ascribe to God the power to operate in the world, which we cannot represent Him to ourselves as doing without setting limits to His infinity, since all work in the world, however vast, is finite. Our knowledge of God's infinity, that is to say of His independence of bounds and limits, is a faith, just as is our belief in our own independence of nature. But we cannot carry this faith into nature and ascribe to God, as so many have been ready to do, a power of doing anything that He pleases there. The dogma that God can do all things is one on which the framers of theological

The inexplicable puzzle offered by the combination of the perfection of God with the imperfection of nature.

systems have often thought themselves at liberty to argue without fear or restraint. But in fact no action at all in a finite world can be ascribed to any agent without imposing limits by the very conception of the action. Nor do we ever find in the Bible that unrestrained licence of inference from the omnipotence of God, and its application to His work in nature, which later systems display. In the Bible many limits and restrictions found in the nature of things, in the nature of man, in the nature of God's own dealings, and of the laws which He has established, come up to qualify the bare statement that God can do all things.

But it is a puzzle only for the intellect.

68. There is no doubt that this involves us in a great puzzle. But it is a puzzle which only presents itself to the intellect. It is hereby proved difficult, or even, let us grant, impossible, to frame a system that shall embrace all the truth about God, man, and nature. But the practical importance of such a difficulty rests upon the question whether we have any reason to expect that we should be able to frame a system that should include in perfect intelligible harmony all that we can know of God, man, and nature. Now there

seems to be no reason why we should presume ourselves entitled to expect any such thing. What is there in man's position in the world towards God and towards nature to render it likely that he would be able to divest his faith of mystery? There is one overwhelming argument against putting forward any such demand: that he cannot get rid of mystery in the very make of his own being. We, who cannot understand ourselves, have but little reason to fancy that we can understand God. But since our want of understanding in our own life is no bar to our faith in the two irreconcilable opposites, human personality and natural law, a similar inability to understand the reconciliation of God's infinity with the bounds of nature cannot be fatal to our belief in a Divine Person as well as in physical causation.

69. The extreme instance of the mystery of God and nature is found in the existence of evil. That awful fact shows us that nature, and God's action in nature, do not reach even to the standard of limited goodness which nature enables us to conceive, and which she partly realises. One hesitates to say that the problem offered by the

Even the existence of evil gives us a God who has the same enemies that we have to contend with.

existence of evil is only one for the intellect and not also for the soul : or that the difficulty under which it places us is but the difficulty of framing a consistent and complete theory. But this at least is true : that the connexion of a perfect Being with an evil world is the counterpart of that bondage of the spirit to the world and the flesh which we experience in ourselves. And accordingly, though evil under a good God be a terrible fact, yet it is far from setting God out of sympathy with us. On the contrary, it is this struggle with evil carried on by Him as well as by man that alone enables us to sympathize truly with Him, or Him to feel for us. Sympathy with the aim and intention of the Author of the world, and with the signs of that intention which are to be discerned in the progress of the world, is the only moral principle which can lift man above selfish considerations and make him yield himself to God. Thus only can we extend to the whole morality of life that loving and self-forgetful interest in the battle which another is fighting, in which every man who has a heart finds his strongest motive to help his brethren in the human sphere. Without this sympathy for the aims of the government of the universe we become the subjects of a lifeless despotism instead of free citizens under a fatherly rule.

70. We need have the less hesitation in maintaining the moral power of sympathy with the designs of God since we find it asserted even in the most unexpected quarters. The authors of systems which might seem deliberately framed to set the First Cause of the universe at an inaccessible distance from the souls of men, and to make fellow-feeling between them impossible and even inconceivable, have been driven in the support of morality to assert that we can discern in things a purpose on the part of their Author with which we are able heartily to sympathise. Thus Mr. Herbert Spencer, in a passage of *The Data of Ethics*, which amounts to a total surrender of agnosticism as a moral system: " If for the Divine Will, supposed to be supernaturally revealed, we substitute the naturally revealed end towards which the Power manifested through evolution works: then since evolution has been and is still working towards the highest life, it follows that conforming to those principles by which the highest life is achieved

And the feeling of sympathy with God is a mighty moral agency even in non-religious systems.

is furthering that end."[1] A power which makes its ends known to us (whether naturally or supernaturally is not the question), and whose ends may be furthered (and by implication may also be hindered) by what we do, is not an unknowable power, but a living God, with whose advancing purpose carried on against opposing powers throughout the history of the world and of man, we are here asked to sympathise and co-operate.

Von Hartmann does not indeed offer to our faith an unknowable Power but an All One, known to be unconscious. One would think that unconsciousness must set the All One still more effectually out of reach of sympathy than Mr. Spencer's creed sets the Unknowable: since we might guess that an Unknowable may perhaps care what we do, but must feel certain that an Unconscious cannot care either about that or anything else. It would not however suit the maintainers of Pessimism to admit this. For as it is their gloomy faith that the world, and especially human life, brings more evil than good, and had better never have existed, it is plain that they can find no argument for living at all, not to say for moral living, within the

[1] *Data of Ethics*, p. 171.

known and conscious world. And if no argument can be brought from beyond the conscious world we shall be bound in reason either to actual suicide, or to that practical suicide which consists in living we care not how: and one of the first duties of man, if any duties he has, will consist in abstaining from propagating a race, the existence of which brings more harm than good to itself and to everything else. Von Hartmann must save himself from a conclusion singularly open to Strauss's taunt, that if the prophets of Pessimism prove that man had better never have lived they thereby prove that themselves had better never have prophesied. Accordingly the last reason by which Pessimism can urge us to live morally or even live at all is found in our sympathy with the Unconscious in the efforts and struggles after a perfect reconciliation of will and idea; to which struggles (singularly unsuccessful as they seem to have hitherto been) this poor world owes its origin and maintenance. This is the moral principle[1] fetched from beyond the

---

[1] Von Hartmann, *Philosophy of the Unconscious*, vol. iii. p. 133 (English translation). "Practical philosophy and life require a positive standpoint, and this is the complete devotion of the personality to the world-process for the sake of its goal, the general

sphere of consciousness which is to counterbalance the Pessimism of the world we know. But it is one of the plainest things possible that by the hypothesis which assigns to the Divinity the title of Unconscious, we are precluded from having any sympathy with it. We cannot embrace a cloud nor yet feel for a stone. We can have sympathy only with the living God, as the Bible is so fond of calling Him: with a God whose relations to nature present that strange union of command and submission in which life as we understand it consists.

71. In every religion which has ever obtained any prevalence among mankind this mysterious opposition between God and the world appears. In some cases it is God in His inscrutable being that seems chiefly to occupy the scene. There

It works also in all great religions, but chiefly in Christianity.

world-redemption. Otherwise expressed, the principle of practical philosophy consists in this, to make the ends of the Unconscious ends of our own consciousness; which follows immediately from the two premises, that in the first place consciousness has made the goal of the world-redemption from the misery of volition its own goal, and secondly that it has the persuasion of the wisdom of the Unconscious, in consequence of which it recognizes all the means made use of by the Unconscious as the most suitable possible, even if in the special case it should be inclined to harbour doubts thereon."—See the clever work of Mr. Barlow, F.T.C.D., entitled *The Ultimatum of Pessimism.*

is a shrinking from bringing Him into contact with the world, and a tendency to find Him through mystical contemplation. Such is the spirit of the great Oriental faiths: yet however far they put back God from the world, He must at some point touch it, or man can have no dealings with Him. Incarnations and earthly symbols bring down the divine nature to contact with material things, and for the mass of worshippers the deity in Himself vanishes wholly from view behind these mundane forms. In the classical systems the earthly and human side of religion forms the first thought, and the nearest to the mind: but behind it is always dimly felt the consciousness of a deeper mystery in the nature of God. But while the mystery lurks in every religion, the character of Christianity is that there is no shrinking from the full recognition of it. There is no attempt to set God apart from the world, or to represent Him as incapable of subjection to the world's laws. It accepts the conditions in the most absolute form, and by a wonderful union of opposites, which human powers could never have invented, it presents God as living among men and for men, exercising His omnipotence for their salvation, but only through a perfection of obedience and submission to the conditions of life and death which was unattainable to them. And all this without ever lowering the spiritual mystery of God's being, or ceasing to place Him above us even while He lives and works beside us.

Here is sympathy with God made truly possible to us through perfection of sympathy in Him for us. This is the completion of that union of our nature with God which is commenced by our creation in His image. We were subjected by Him to vanity, as S. Paul expresses the incomprehensible slavery of spiritual beings to a material world. But here is fulfilled to us the "hope" which the apostle finds in our subjection, instead of seeing in it as others do the despairing certainty that we are enslaved for ever, and that no true mastery can ever come of our wrestling with nature and her awful powers.

Religion meets a natural want in man which a habit of questioning may dull, as it does other human affections.

72. But all of this kind that can be said is but a necessarily imperfect attempt to reproduce in reflection the nature of that attraction of religion for man which in all ages he has spontaneously

felt. The more one regards this universal attraction, the more one doubts whether its significance has been grasped by our men of science. Cultivated in intellect to the highest point, such men find religion too high and difficult for their acceptance—it lies beyond them. They protest that after searching the universe with their observations, calculating its forces with their understanding, and feeling all the sentiments of wonder and admiration which it is fitted to excite, they do not find God. Could one have supposed that beliefs too mystical for the cultivated would have been found welcome to the common mind, bound down to what can be seen and touched? If indeed religion had consisted in earthly observances, and depended upon natural terrors, we might not have thought its prevalence so strange: but it is certain that if religion had relied only upon these material influences it would soon have been trodden down and lost in the crush and struggle for existence. Men do not show themselves so obstinate in retaining even the best founded fears, as for instance that of death; nor in practising any earthly observances which cannot show their practical utility in the most undeniable form.

How comes it then that they have so universally believed a religion? How comes it that religion, instead of showing itself in highly cultivated minds and being lost in those of the vulgar and the unimaginative, is far more apt to display the contrary characteristics? Millions who are bound within the narrower circles of knowledge and sentiment have agreed to feel after God and to find Him; while the cultivated few seem often to lose both the longing after Him and the power to discern Him.

Explanations of this fact, very flattering to the superiority of the philosophic mind, may doubtless be offered. But there is an explanation, not so tender to the pride of intellect, sufficient to account for the phenomena: that there is an essential fitness in religion for meeting an original capacity and want in the mind of man, which grows dull through the exclusive pursuit of science. This capacity and want it may be impossible to prove or to explain: it is impossible to prove or to explain any of the essential tendencies of human nature. And it may become dull and vanish from view when the mind assumes an attitude of persistent questioning: this is the case with all the affections, even the most undeniable and essential.

All the affections grow dull in individuals, and even in whole classes and generations, which are intellectually cultivated to an abnormal degree. If we desire to test or understand the natural force of any of the original affections we must assume an attitude of faith and feeling, or study the phenomena in those to whom such an attitude is possible. And the defenders of religion must not be accused of disrespect to the intellect, if they believe that an incapacity of the intellect may exist in religion to the same extent and for the same reason that it exists in regard to the affections. When we attempt to describe any of our affections or tastes, we are ever conscious that we have failed.[1] The fervour and reality of it exhale and vanish as we try to describe it, for the attitude of our mind in reflection and in statement, like that of our hearer's in listening and judging, is entirely different from that of feeling and acting. If he should be unsympathising and sceptical, he will be able to prove to his own perfect satisfaction that

> I cannot teach
> My hand to hold my spirit so far off
> From myself—me—that I should bring thee proof
> In words of love hid in me out of reach.
> E. B. BROWNING, *Sonnets from the Portuguese.*

the feeling and its object were imaginary and unnecessary; and he is likely enough to be able to persuade us that his view of the case is just. And even should he sympathise to the highest possible degree, the intellectual reproduction will be but a cold and unreal image of a feeling which was real and rested upon a true object.

73. We have found ourselves obliged to confess that our knowledge of man as a person rests, like these tastes and affections, upon an intuition which can be recognised and accepted by the mind, but not proved to a doubter, and which it is easy to disbelieve. But the light vanishes out of life when we disbelieve it: for though our intercourse with the beauty and variety of things is a source of high delight to us, yet by itself it does not satisfy the soul. It leads up to communion with man, and without this all is imperfect. In personal communion all other communion finds its completion, and the want of it is capable of depriving every beauty which the rest of the world can offer of its charm. Imagination, indeed, endows the trees and flowers and the lovely scenes of nature with personality: they seem to speak to us and to

Fifth step. The natural desire to meet personality everywhere.

be partakers in what we feel. But this is only imagination, and it could never have been felt, or, if felt, been sustained, unless the longing after personal communion had been fed by constant contact with those beings who have in reality the wondrous character which is only imagined in nature. If a man be really set in permanence apart from his fellow-men, nature loses its personality and therewith its charm. The same is true of the lower animals. We make friends of them, and it sometimes seems as if they were almost human; yet they are not so, and we could not imagine them to be so if the true personal intercourse which we can have with man did not constantly sustain the idea within us. We are always calling our dogs and other animal favourites by human names, addressing to them sentences of human language and otherwise treating them as if they were human beings, to an extent which, as we are perfectly well aware, is unwarranted by what we know of their real mental constitution.

This desire to add personality to every kind of pleasure is testified by our constant wish to share with other human minds the delight which we have in the world. To be able to enjoy beautiful scenery or intercourse with favourite animals alone and solitary, is unnatural and when it occurs we count it at least an eccentricity. The natural habit is that you should never enjoy any external thing thoroughly and completely unless you have some friend by your side to enjoy it with you. Wordsworth seemed to delight in solitary communion with nature, but it was only that he might devise the forms of thought and expression by which he should call a thousand readers to share his delight. And if nature seems sometimes to afford us a welcome shelter from man, that is but a passing phase of feeling, and results from our having experienced in man something very different from what man ought to render to us.

A large part of our delight in art seems to be the result of the same longing after personal communion. It is strange that we derive from the picture of a beautiful thing, imperfect though the reproduction must be, a kind of pleasure which we do not feel from gazing upon the thing itself: and that even things which are not beautiful in themselves are capable of conferring keen pleasure when they appear in some skilful picture. This shows that we are framed to regard everything which bears signs of having been passed through a personal mind, with intensified delight; as if nothing, however fair, was the same to us without the mark of personality upon it as when it bears that stamp. And art must recognise this principle. If it strives for mere imitative reproduction it is but a poor thing. It must select and interpret and explain nature, and give us its productions with the marks of creative intention and will.

74. This irresistible longing after personal communion bears every mark of having been impressed upon the mind of man by its Author. This we may say without the most distant intention to deny the doctrine of evolution. *The desire has the stamp of evolution.* If the chief apostle of evolution himself is, as we have seen, permitted to speak of the "naturally revealed end towards which the power manifested in creation works," why should we be denied the liberty of recognising in the ends of evolution the purpose of God? The mind of man is, so far as we can see, the crown and summit of evolution and that which lies deepest and works most strongly in the mind of man must be regarded as the issue towards which evolution tends. Where shall we find any tendency that is more deeply

P

impressed upon man than the longing for personal communion, or any object for which man can better be said to exist than that of the recognition of personality in the outer world? And even if, as extreme evolutionists are ready to maintain, we must put aside entirely all recognition of final causes and of a purpose discernible in the progress of things, we are not therefore obliged to set aside the great fact in human nature on which we have been dwelling. It remains a fact, howsoever the fact arises, that man can nowhere be content without personal communion with others. So he is framed and fashioned. And he cannot make himself another being than this. He can contradict or ignore this characteristic of his nature only at the same cost at which any essential want may be denied, namely, misery.

75. Now, if the desire for personal intercourse drives us all our life long to the company of our fellow-men, to delight in recognising their presence and their work, and a longing to find personality even where it does not really exist, it is impossible that the desire should be fully satisfied by any communion that we can find in the natural world.

And demands a higher satisfaction than it receives here.

Though the satisfaction which the craving meets in our intercourse with men be very great, yet it is never absolutely complete: it always manifests itself as a desire partly unsatisfied even in presence of the best supply that the world can afford to it. We never can have such satisfaction in personal communion as does not make us long after more of it and deeper. Nay, the awakening of spiritual longings which cannot be satisfied is often the characteristic effect upon us of the best earthly communion, and the point in which it excels that intercourse with men which is ordinary and superficial.

How imperfect is the best communion of man with man! For how short a time it lasts and how small a part of life it covers! Although sympathy with other spirits is so fitted to add delight to every experience of nature and art that the best we can enjoy in this sort is all imperfect without it, yet few of us command the truest sympathy on the part of other human minds: and if we have it we are hardly able to enjoy the treasure, and very soon we lose it. Such are the conditions of our existence that we are obliged to live most of our lives and to gain most of our experience alone, to the maiming of life and the loss of the best uses of experience. Life as a whole is but imperfect and consists of commencements rather than accomplished ends; the best things it gives are only fitted to be foretastes of something better, to keep alive our longing for a life that shall be fuller of satisfaction and of usefulness, and that shall not be cut short by death. If this be the general condition of life, we cannot wonder that it should be specially observable in that personal intercourse which is the very essence of life: and that here especially we should find great happiness indeed, and great power of usefulness and profit, but all marked with imperfection, a promise rather than a fulfilment.

This longing after better and higher personal communion than this world can give is not the unhealthy discontent of minds that will not make the best use of what they have. No one who considers the spiritual history of mankind with attention can fail to see that it is those who have best used, both for their own happiness and for the benefit of others, the gifts of personal intercourse on earth, who have also longed most for intercourse with divine persons, more intimately enjoyed than the earthly, and extended beyond this life. They have not complained of any poverty in the blessings of companionship with their fellows here. It is the very blessedness of the earthly communion that has both made them long for the higher and believe that the Powers who conferred the one must have the other in store. The desire to see personal communion extended everywhere, so that there shall not be a single pleasure enjoyed by man with which the sense of one who sympathises with it shall not mingle, stands in close connection with the mental conviction that the fellowship of human beings is a real gift, the existence of which requires to be accounted for; and is best accounted for by the belief that it flows from the divine cause who Himself gives us in communion with Himself that of which human intercourse is the image.

76 If the faith in our own personality, in the power of our will, the command of our conscience, and the struggle with the world which personality imposes, find their explanation in God, the power of man to commune with man, the personality of men

The power of personal communion between man and man, and the desire after extension of this communion, finds its cause and source in God.

considered not individually but in its mysterious commerce with other men, must have an explanation too. There must be some higher power which confers the wonderful gift of communion upon men and forms the medium in which it is carried on. That we are one in Him is a truth which is capable both of a natural and a supernatural application. And the whole character of human fellowship is explained by the character of God, who enables His children to understand and feel for each other in a fashion too mysterious for unconscious nature wholly to explain.

And so it comes that the same want of the human soul which leads it through nature to man, leads it through man to God. Of earthly powers that which is highest in man is his brotherhood with men. And this is the part of human life which best reflects God and most clearly points to Him. For the best human personality is on a level with ourselves, and with all its helpfulness and happiness it only meets us in the same fashion in which we meet it; and how poor we feel that to be. We are left longing for a personality which bears to our own the relation not merely of a helper but of a source and origin, and which has known and loved us before ever we knew or loved it. And though many signs of God are found in the individual life it is the life of man with man which has been most powerful to lead him to the divine source of love.

VI.

GOD REVEALED.

"Call no man your father upon the earth, for one is your Father, which is in heaven."—S. MATT. xxiii. 9.

"We, being many, are one body in Christ."—ROM. xii. 5.

"Because ye are sons, God hath sent forth the Spirit of His Son into your hearts, crying, Abba, Father."—GAL. iv. 6.

77. At the first glance it seems strange that while man can understand so many things he should not be able to understand himself. And yet upon reflection it is not so strange. For the knowledge how to work with an instrument is a different thing from the knowledge of its construction: and the man who is engaged in working the instrument is not of necessity the most likely person to explain its mechanism. We are instruments

Knowledge of man is not merely knowledge of the instruments he works with but of himself.

constructed for a practical purpose, namely life in the world. And our mechanism has been adapted to that end, adjusted and enlarged, as the evolutionists tell us, according to the practical needs and occasions of an immense lapse of time. There has been nothing in this history calculated to train man in reflection upon his own origin, or upon his own nature and powers, except so far as they are the instruments with which he has to work. And in this point of view they hold the same external position to him which the rest of nature does. It is no wonder that many men should spend their whole mental lives among externals, and that some should turn this habit into a philosophy and assert that the knowledge of the positive history of his own states of mind is the only knowledge of himself that is possible for man.

And yet there must be another knowledge. Besides his knowledge of his instrument the workman must have a knowledge of his own power to work it, and, therefore, of his own existence as separate from it. The knowledge can not be formally stated; it can be used only for practical purposes and in connection with work. Yet it is plain that this knowledge must be implied in every moment of work, and that if the artisan were to lose it his work would stop. Moreover, it is a knowledge which is capable of varieties in intensity, and according as it is stronger or weaker the efficiency of the worker will grow or relax. The belief that we ourselves are something different from our bodies and from our minds is in its very nature mysterious, and may even be called an absurdity by persons unwilling to accept mysteries. But if we accept as a working hypothesis the belief that we have the command over both body and mind, and therefore must not identify ourselves with them, it is confirmed by every practical test. Our powers, both material and mental, array themselves obediently under the command of the self when it asserts its command. Whereas if we determine to believe that we are nothing except a bundle of faculties the theory cannot be put into practice. An army without a general, or an engine without a driver, are faint images to express what a bundle of faculties would be without any I myself to command them. There must, therefore, be a self: and the confidence with which we make this assertion shows that we are conscious of a knowledge of the self. We know it as a mystery, but we know it. We cannot prove it, or even put it into a form of definition which is capable of being submitted to the process of proof. It belongs to those original principles which must be accepted as the bases of all reasoning, and for that very cause must themselves be accepted without being proved.

The knowledge which we have of the personality of other men partakes of the same character as that which we have of our own. When we ascribe to them the property of personality we must take the very meaning which we attribute to the word from our own consciousness. We are conscious that our powers and attributes of mind and body, whether original or acquired, would not if added together constitute our whole self; but that we must also, and chiefly, take account of an indescribable some one who is possessor of all these faculties, or, if you will, is possessed by them, but at all events is not they. And if we believe that other men are like ourselves we must hold the same opinion concerning them: that the process of adding together all their faculties and attributes, and what we know of them externally and historically, would not make the whole of what we know them to be. We must also hold them to be constituted not only of faculties but of the same mysterious and unknowable self behind the faculties which we find in ourselves. This cannot be proved concerning them. For the very nature of this inward part shuts it up from proof. It cannot be placed upon the table to demonstrate that it exists, nor dissected to show what it is made of. But if we have faith to believe that our fellow-men are not machines but selves and persons, and to act upon the belief, it is found to answer. Men respond to personal treatment as they never respond to any dead force.

Therefore, in spite of all difficulties, we claim that we know our fellow-men to possess personality. And we know them not merely in theory but practically. There is a kind and degree of sympathy or fellow feeling which is peculiar to personal beings in their intercourse with each other, and partakes of the same mysterious and indescribable character that belongs to the nature of such beings. So that although we can never know other people explicitly as subjects, or in their own intimate self-consciousness, yet something of a subjective nature enters our knowledge of them in the way of feeling if not of intellectual perception. In one sense we cannot know even ourselves as subjects; for as soon as we contemplate ourselves we become objects to our minds; and yet we know ourselves subjectively so far as this, that we know that the feelings we experience must have a subject, and from experiencing the feeling we know something of the self which it affects. And the same way of knowledge extends to other people also, and we know not merely their feelings, but know them as they feel. And although this language may seem to some people forced, and even, perhaps, meaningless, yet if they were asked whether other people may not make us one with themselves, and whether we cannot make them one with ourselves in a way in which no impersonal thing can ever be, they would probably assent.

78. We have been led through the knowledge of ourselves and of other men up to the knowledge of God. Like the others, the knowledge of God is one which depends on faith. The idea of

And our knowledge of God is of similar character: subjective as well as objective.

God cannot be defined. It cannot be proved.[1] The utmost the understanding can do is to prove the want of Him: to show the blank place which remains in nature if we do not suppose Him, and the futile and unaccountable character which belongs to the spiritual conditions and history of mankind unless He be a reality. But it is the power of communion with persons involved in the possession of personality which accepts the faith in Him as a supreme practical necessity: as a fact without which we not merely cannot explain our own existence but cannot exist.

We know God not merely objectively as the maker of the universe, but subjectively, as united with the self in which all our faculties inhere, and to which all our experiences belong. God has

[1] "Thou canst not prove the nameless, O my son,
Nor canst thou prove the world thou movest in;
Thou canst not prove that thou art body alone,
Nor canst thou prove that thou art spirit alone,
Nor canst thou prove that thou art both in one.
Thou canst not prove thou art immortal, no,
Nor yet that thou art mortal—nay, my son,
Thou canst not prove that I who speak with thee
Am not thyself in converse with thyself—
For nothing worthy proving can be proven
Nor yet disproven. Wherefore if thou be wise,
Cleave ever to the sunnier side of doubt,
And cling to faith beyond the forms of faith."
 TENNYSON, *The Ancient Sage.*

never been set forth among mankind, at least by any of His true prophets, in the Church or out of it, as being external to man in the same sense in which nature is. "In Him we live and move and have our being," could not be said of anything wholly external. He is both within us and without: He is both one with us and different from us. And the inward knowledge of Him comes to us through the outward and along with it.[1]

79. An outward origin of inward faith characterises our self-knowledge and our knowledge of mankind. We can know nothing intellectually except through the forms which our minds can grasp. But there comes to us through these forms a knowledge of something which the mind cannot grasp. It may be truly said that all acts and words of ourselves and of other men are revelations, as bringing us in contact with the personal agent behind them, whom without them we could not know and whom we never can fully comprehend even with their help.

<small>*Revelation the only means of knowing either man or God.*</small>

---

[1] "Wir mussten den 'Weltwillen' seinem Wesen nach von vornherein in einer Doppeltheit erfassen, nämlich als transcendent und immanent zu gleicher zeit. . . . Somit fällt denn hier unser Weltwille mit der ewigen Gottheit selbst zusammen."—PETERS, pp. 352, 353.

In like manner God can never be known except by revelation: and every fact in nature or in history by which we know God partakes of the character of revelation. It is a misleading use of the term revelation which confines it to historical incidents alone; as if nature also did not both reveal God and also fail to reveal Him just as the events in history do. Both in nature and in history we learn to know Him, but in both He is declared as one whom 'no man hath seen at any time,' as one whom 'no man hath seen or can see.' For there is in both the external world and in history an element of contingency and limitation essential to their very nature, even apart from the discovery of imperfection according to earthly standards. The infinite God cannot be manifested by them. The contrast, the opposition which exists between facts existing in time and space and the eternal personality of God is essential and would exist even if they were the most perfect revelations which facts are capable of being. No essential difference in the terms of the problem is made by the assertion or denial of the perfection of nature or of the plenary inspiration of the Bible or the infallibility of the Church.

Yet without revelation made through facts God cannot be known any more than man. The understanding must open the way before that mysterious faculty within us can come into exercise and tell of the presence of personality. And all attempts to realise personality except in connection with the living history in which it is displayed at work must be abstract and lifeless. It is in the play of feeling and life that personality comes to view. In the struggles and affections of life our own inner nature shows itself. Through the infinite variety of circumstances and the action and reaction of our organism and environment we learn that there is something in ourselves beyond our organism. The freedom and the power of our real self is known to be present. And the like is true of the human personalities around us. We know them in action and in life, and thus only. It follows that neither our own personality nor that of our neighbours can ever be known except under some *form*. The form is that idea level and comprehensible to our mental faculties which embodies in itself the series of facts through which we know ourselves or our friends. And underneath the form lies, as we always feel, an incomprehensible subject the same through all changes. Thus the form of each man's existence is found in the characteristics and peculiarities of his body and mind and circumstances. These things constitute his individuality, and they may vary and change in infinite ways. But his personality is that abiding subject which retains its identity through all changes and which he denotes by the word I.

80. If discussion about human nature becomes empty and uninteresting unless it concerns itself with the various forms of life, which indeed alone change it from a dead thing into a living, the same must needs hold in religion. And this is a disadvantage under which religion is constantly placed when the question of its evidence is discussed. The question is often argued in the abstract without any reference to the contents of religion, in which alone its living interest for man is found; while at the same time human nature is displayed in the condition of wanting religion, but not in the better and more attractive condition in which the want is filled with the fulness of God.

Emptiness of religious discussions apart from the facts of God's self-revelation.

The want of religion which human nature displays, were it ever so fully proved, can never in its negative character as a want, prove religion true. It may prove that man can never be happy without a religion; it may prove religion so necessary to the highest sentiments and the best morality that the beneficial nature of truth to man shall seem very doubtful, if it be truth to teach that there is no foundation for religion. It may reduce human life, in the absence of religion, to something so poor and disappointing, whether to the individual or the race, that it is not worth living and had better never have been given. Yet all these miseries might be our destiny : a want does not prove the existence of its own supply. But the want of religion considered as a fact in human history continued through a vast number of ages with the utmost persistence and in spite of vast discouragements, assumes more than a negative character. A want is in one point of view a positive phenomenon, an active exertion of human faculties in wishing and striving. And the obstinately maintained action of human nature in keeping alive the want of religion is no mean proof that there is positive truth in religion. For the most obvious account of the persistence of the want is that enough of supply has been received to keep the want living. Mendicants do not ply their calling for years in a desert where there are no givers. And we may be sure that if the prayers and cravings of religion had for so many thousand ages been uttered to mere emptiness, and had received no answer addressed to either the inward or the outward faculties of man, they would long since have ceased to be felt and have vanished as functions having no use.

But although the religious wants and cravings of humanity have their positive side and form no uninteresting subject of treatment both in history and in fiction to this very day, yet a more fruitful subject and better fitted to make religion acceptable, is its fitness to supply these wants and cravings, and to satisfy man's mind and heart. Now the wants which above all urge men to religion are those which are fostered by their experience of their nature, and by their intercourse with one another. Men cannot satisfy themselves that they are filling their due place in nature or exerting their due influence, unless they ascribe to themselves personality: a free and ruling power over nature, and especially over their own natural faculties and powers. And they cannot satisfy themselves that they know their fellow men in their true character so long as they consider them as mere parts of nature like the inanimate world: they must find persons among the things of the world and personal action exerted through the things of the world, or life will seem to them empty. Their want in religion is the same carried higher.

81. What form of religion shall we select in order to try whether the habits of mind which are fostered amidst human personalities can find in a divine faith that larger exercise which they crave? Whether we believe or not, we can have little doubt in naming the religion which we may most fitly choose for an example. *The Catholic faith is the form of religion in which the question whether religion satisfies the wants of our personality may best be tested.* The Catholic faith must be fairly owned to have best shown what religion can be and do for men. It has prevailed among the highest races and marked its power by the most beneficent results. Those that take refuge in religion from doubt almost always select this form of it. And there are comparatively

very few who change the Catholic for any other form of faith, however many there may be who forsake it and others for unbelief. But we must remember that the Catholic religion contemplates other forms with no contempt. It regards them as yielding imperfectly that which it gives in purity and completeness.

The Catholic faith is this, that we worship one God in Trinity and Trinity in Unity, neither confounding the Persons nor dividing the substance. The essence of Catholic doctrine was held in the most important ages of the Church's life to consist in the maintenance of the creed of the divine personality; and all other questions were regarded as subsidiary to this. For personality fills as important a part in theology as it does in human life. Communion with God as a Person is the essence of religion, and the divine personality must needs be the most important subject of the Church's thought. Her decisions on the subject rest confessedly upon an inscrutable mystery. She cannot understand the Godhead, and she does not encourage her children to believe that they can do so. She can but record the facts which are revealed in Scripture and in her own traditions and in the experiences of that divine life of the soul which her members live, and which she sums up and represents. Every sentiment in the mind of any man must rest upon a truth, or a belief supposed true, which the mind explicitly or implicitly holds; much more must a religious life of peculiar stamp and character, bringing with it the renunciation of many apparent advantages and spreading through a vast mass of human minds of all classes and degrees, rest upon adequate truths. It is impossible that a spiritual life so entirely different from that which the visible world and the powers of nature have ever produced could be fostered in man without a conviction of the firmest character that relations exist for him beyond nature. Nothing dreamy, or indefinite, or merely sentimental, or manufactured by the imagination without reality behind it, is adequate to be the foundation of such a superstructure. And in the Catholic creed we find the Church's expression of what she found revealed and accepted with the assent of her whole spiritual consciousness as the truth on which the new life of Christianity must be built. It is a praise which would perhaps have been rejected by the objects of it, yet is probably well founded, that the authorities of the Church in their doctrinal decrees were not so exclusively moved by the weight of authority as they believed themselves to be. The aptness of the faith to be the support of Christian life and its fitness to supply the wants of humanity co-operated with deference to authority, and imparted the warmth and earnestness to its advocates which mere conservatism and the attachment to old forms never could have given.

82. Now there must be some great reason in the nature of things which procured for this creed the acceptance and power which it possesses. And it seems no improbable account of the matter to believe that it has carried out and satisfied in the spiritual sphere those habits and tendencies which are fostered in man by his experience of life and his intercourse with other men. Personality in the divine nature is accepted as a general truth, because it explains to man how personality exists at all in the world, and because it satisfies the desire after personal communion which is the most powerful affection of man's mind and heart. And it would be a probable and sufficient explanation

Why has this creed met with such acceptance and exercised such power?

of the welcome which the Catholic creed has met if we were to find that it explains the existence of the most essential forms under which personal communion exists between man and man, and satisfies in a higher and eternal sphere the habits which those forms of human communion impress upon the heart of man so deeply and so strongly as to become a part of its very frame.

We know that a human personality existing alone is inconceivable, and would form no specimen of humanity, any more than a brick would form a specimen of a house. While we know the personality of other men only as the reflection of our own, we are made aware of our own and educated in the practical use of it, only by contact with them. Although in the logical order our knowledge of our own personality precedes our knowledge of that of other men, yet it is not so in the order of time. Our consciousness of ourselves and of other persons come together into being under the pressure of the experience of life, and in the forms which life prescribes and imposes. Life in its experiences teaches us imperceptibly but irresistibly through every moment from birth to death, and fills us with the prepossessions, the anticipations, the bent and habit which we must perforce carry into every state into which we can come. Opinions adopted in later days are but weak and ineffectual agents in eradicating the mental tendencies which all life from the first has impressed on us; and in life the chief element by far is personal intercourse. This is the true educator of man. Philosophers and preachers are alike powerless in comparison to the daily teaching of personal communion between man and man, and still more between child and man; and their comparative impotence is not less conspicuous when they meet with assent than when they are rejected. Habits of thought and tendencies of affection which have grown through our earliest experience, and been inherited from countless ages before, assert themselves in spite of all adopted opinions. The latter are only heresies—theories taken up by the mind; the former are of the very make of the soul, which it did not voluntarily assume, and which it cannot cast away. When we think over this truth which the doctrines of development have brought into great prominence, it seems that no more impossible supposition can be conceived than this; that a being framed and educated to find in personal communion the crown and completion of all the experiences of his life, his guidance and his happiness alike, should be able to look beyond the world into that invisible sphere which presses so closely upon him, and be satisfied to find there, not the personal presence which is the highest thing in human life, but the dead unconsciousness which he here knows as the mark not of persons but of things. And if man seeks personality and will have it in the spiritual world, he must seek it in the forms which are the inseparable clothing of it here.

83. How then shall we discern the essential forms under which personality meets us in life, so as to be able to pronounce what that religion is which reflects this experience in the completest way? We know that in various descriptions of polytheism there has been a transfer on the most lavish scale of the forms of human personality into religion. Every trade and profession, every city and community, every virtue, and sometimes every vice, which existed among men, had among the gods its representative, which embodied its idea in a more intense and permanent form than was to

It corresponds to the essential forms under which personality meets us in life.

be found in humanity. These were corrupt religions: but they were the corruptions of the great truth that as man and man's life is the chief work of God, so man and his life must be the chief revelation of God. The principle as used in polytheism assumed excessively capricious forms without any warrant in revealed facts. God had declared Himself to men, St. Paul believed, but they changed the glory of the incorruptible God into an image made like to corruptible man. Man must be more humble and self-restrained in his observations of God's teaching impressed on human life, if he is really to find there any anticipation of what God is.

But it is not difficult for us to find the true method. In order to discover the genuine impress and reflection of God in human life, we must leave out all the corruptions and unessential developments of humanity, and go back to the purest and simplest elements of existence common to all men at all stages of progress, and in which all minds are moulded by the universal necessities of the case. And these we find in the primary relations of the family.

Man wakens to a sense of his own personality to

find a father above him and brothers beside him; the mother and the sisters repeating the same relations in a subordinate form. The father above, the brother beside, and the self within: human nature cannot exist in more elementary forms than these. Man would not be what he is if personality were not found in these forms. They are the spiritual mould into which the soul of every man is run, and they give it a shape which can never be changed. It is impossible that the soul should not retain through all its existence the impressions of the fatherly and brotherly relations as well as its self-consciousness. Those impressions are inherited from an innumerable series of progenitors, and they are repeated in the individual experience of every life. If the primary natural form of the relationships be not present in a father and brothers by blood, there is provision for substitutes where it is wanting, as there is for extensions where it is present. From the original elements an infinite variety of personal life is developed without introducing any relation essentially new. From fatherhood come all those relations of man to his fellows which imply protection, correction, or command on one side, and reverence on the other, as the king, the judge, the elder; and from the brother come all that imply mutual familiarity, helpfulness, and example, while in ourselves we find that personal consciousness whereby we are one with our fathers and brothers, and become fathers and brothers in our turn. These great root ideas of the human race combined in an unlimited number of various aspects make up life and furnish the spiritual clothing of the soul, which is trained among them. To this common language and common feeling testify. What more common than to extend to those above us the ways of speech and feeling which find their first application to the father; and to call mankind brothers when we regard them as on the same level with ourselves. And how deep lies the sense of communion, nay, of identity, between us and them. These are the forms of personality which make us what we are. They exercise their influence over us unceasingly and from the beginning to the end of life. They demand of us the recognition of fatherly and brotherly relations as held by others to ourselves, and the exercise of the same relations by us to others when the occasion comes. The due use and application of these ideas constitute all right doing between man and man. There is no form of virtue from the commonest to the most devoted which it is possible for us to practice towards one another that will not fall under the true conception of these relations, nor any form of offence which is not an infringement of them.

84. But while these are the elements of human life, we have the bitterest experience how far human life falls short of exemplifying all that they might be. How far the earthly father is from being what he ought to be to his children; he is wanting alike in love and wisdom. Even in the very best instances he does not guide nor protect nor correct his children to their profit, but to his pleasure; and multitudes of cases occur in which he shows himself absolutely neglectful of any such duty. Brotherhood meets a realisation equally imperfect. There is indeed so much both of it and of fatherhood as imparts to the words father and brother a wealth of delightful association which speaks of love, help, and union. Yet, though we call mankind our brother men, how much there is of enmity and injury, and of every-

The failures of human life to fill up and complete its own forms.

thing that is unbrotherly in the conduct of man to man. How little of that self-sacrifice in which alone brotherly duty is complete. While the father is less than a true father to us, and the brother less than a true brother, we are still more sensible of the failures of our inward self to be either true son or true brother, or true to that duty to self from which all others spring.

Even if all were otherwise in the moral aspects of life, none of these relations could ever be completely realised on earth, because brotherhood and fatherhood (as the New Testament says of human priesthood) 'could not continue by reason of death.' Death carries off even him who best realises the idea of human life, and leaves behind those whose existence was bound up with and completed by his, all maimed and imperfect.

And thus life is a training and education of the self,—first in the enjoyment of sonship and brotherhood and the sense of all that properly belongs to these personal relations, and secondly in the sense of the world's deficiency in both. Training and education are indeed words too weak to express the whole truth of the case. For what we call training and education cannot begin until life and its faculties are developed, and they are an anxious and deliberate proceeding. But these relations of which we are speaking consist in the nature of things, and teach their lessons the more effectually because they require no deliberate attempt or intention either in tutor or learner. They pass imperceptibly and irresistibly into the very constitution of the soul, and it is impossible for us, whatever beliefs or opinions we may chance to take up, to lose the aspirations and the desires which have thus been rooted in us. Not one of those habits or impulses of the mind which drive men to seek for scientific truth is so deeply engrained in our nature, and so impossible to check or resist, as that which urges men to follow personality, and to find it under the forms of which we have been speaking. If we are to judge of the importance of a principle in human life by the numbers of mankind who display it in action, or by the persistence and energy with which it works within them, we must confess that the longing for personal intercourse and the longing that it should be all that it might be, is immeasurably in advance of the longing for scientific truth.

85. As in our experience of facts of all kinds

we are driven to seek a cause underlying the things which we see and experience, so we are impelled to look behind the fatherhood, and brotherhood, and the self-consciousness, which are displayed in human life, for a cause which makes them what they are and gives them that place in man's soul which they possess. This demand of the mind combines itself with the wants of the heart. As every disappointment of a desire which has a deep and important place in our hearts leaves a longing that influences our whole life, so it cannot be but that the constant and necessary inadequacy of human personalities to fulfil their own idea shall exercise an abiding influence upon the ruling desires of all mankind.

The forms of the Divine Personality are at once the cause and the completion of the human.

Since this is the history of the formation of human minds, and the habit which the constitution of their earthly existence forces them to contract, we can well understand the welcome which the Catholic faith has received among them. For it represents the father and the brother and the self as eternally and perfectly existing. It tells men that as all nature, and man the crown of nature, have their origin in God who is their cause, and reveal Him, so there is something in God distinctly corresponding to the forms in which mankind necessarily exists, and these forms therefore, when regarded in their spiritual aspect, reveal God. It is indeed only in a mystery that this divine truth can be grasped by the mind. But this can furnish no good or sufficient reason for doubt, so long as men must acknowledge that their own personality and that of their fellows is a mystery to them no less than that of God.

Such a revelation is welcomed by the reason of men as shewing in the first cause of their life something which accounts for the forms which life assumes in them. If indeed we were to regard man as a purely physical phenomenon, his personality as a physical product, and the relations of his personality to others and the feelings consequent on those relations as all physical circumstances, we should then need no other account of the matter than that which physical evolution affords. But the universal reason of mankind has not accepted a physical view of life. To it the spiritual aspects of human existence have seemed as essential as the material, and require as adequate an account of their origin. The close connexion of mental development with physical has been brought out of late with emphasis: and indeed experience always taught men that mind and body were closely connected and that the condition of the former was greatly dependent on that of the latter. It was known that the forms of our life were found in their outward and material aspects in the lower animals. Yet this close union with matter does not seem to mankind in general to deprive mind and spirit of their proper character, or to account for them by physical causes as if they were phenomena of matter. The affections of human nature, the obedience and the self-sacrifice which are drawn out by human connexions, have led men to believe that there is something in the source of our being which exemplifies in itself these qualities and therefore produces them in us. And if we ask for a spiritual and personal cause of our spiritual and personal existence it must needs be welcome to reason that we should recognise in it the same forms which are essential to personality in ourselves.

But it is not by reasoning that the mass of mankind are governed. It is not from reasoning that even the few who can reason derive their strongest impulses, or those which abide with them most persistently. But wherever there is a heart which has experienced the power of the name father, and the appeal which it makes to our faith and our affections; wherever a want can be felt which an earthly father cannot supply, or a hope entertained which an earthly father must disappoint: there is to be found the capacity of believing in a Father in heaven and the feeling how sorely He is needed. Whenever any one wants the aid of a brother, or through feeling how much his brethren can do for him is led to feel how much they cannot do: there is room for faith in the eternal Brother whose self-sacrifice is perfect and whose help is all-sufficient. Whenever a man feels the deficiency of will and of vigour in his own secret self, and longs for some addition of strength from those mysterious regions in which the wonderful powers which he already possesses have their rise: there is the need for the Holy Ghost and a reason for believing in Him. Now there is no human being so deeply sunk in ignorance or apathy as not to have a dim feeling of such wants in him, nor any so cultured and so strong as to be independent of these desires and hopes.

86. The Catholic faith was proclaimed to men thus prepared by nature. But no part of the proof of its truth was rested on any want of theirs. It told of an eternal Father expressly revealed under that familiar name, the true Author of our being, in comparison to whom the earthly medium by which our life was given hardly deserves the title: our Protector, our Teacher, our Ruler, our Maintainer, performing in perfection all those duties of fatherhood of which men are the imperfect agents. He is never absent, and He is never to die. He encompasses our whole life, and presents within the very depths of our nature that call for dependence, trust, and obedience which comes to us not unreally, but fitfully and imperfectly, from our fathers in the flesh. It reveals a Son of God in the true nature of His Father as earthly sons are of theirs, able therefore to bring His brethren to the very bosom of their common Father. And this Son of God is Son of Man, and not ashamed to call men brethren. He does for them the true duties of brotherhood

In this character the Catholic faith was proclaimed and accepted.

as men never do them. His example is perfect, whether on the side that turns towards the common Father or on that which regards men themselves. He sacrificed Himself for His brethren that He might bring them to their Father, and that He might fill them with that true brotherhood which will lead them to sacrifice themselves for Him and for His brother men. And it reveals a Spirit who can reach our spirit, that is our inmost self, and draw it to the Father and to the Son. "Because ye are sons God hath sent forth the Spirit of his Son into your hearts whereby ye cry, Abba Father. The Spirit itself beareth witness with our spirit, that we are the children of God: and if children, then heirs; heirs of God and joint-heirs with Christ." And again, "For this cause I bow my knees unto the Father, from whom every fatherhood in heaven and earth is named, that He would grant you according to the riches of His glory, that ye may be strengthened with power through His Spirit in the inward man: that Christ may dwell in your hearts through faith, to the end that ye being rooted and grounded in love may be strong to apprehend with all the saints what is the breadth, and length, and height, and depth, and to know the love of Christ which passeth knowledge that ye may be filled unto all the fulness of God."

Thus the Catholic faith covers the whole personal life of man, and extends the range of his personal communion, always upon the same great lines which life establishes for him from the first. If additional examples were wanting of the analogy, or rather the unity, thus established between life and religion we might find it in this: that many of the derivative applications which we find in earthly experience to rise out of the great constituent elements of personal life are found also in religion. The Father is the judge, the ruler, the teacher: the Brother is the leader, the captain, the king. And as in the earthly relationships, the idea of fatherhood and brotherhood, distinct though they be, are yet not so separate but that the functions of the one often pass to the other; so also it is in the faith: command is not so purely the office of the father, nor obedience and reverence so exclusively his due, but that both may pass to the brother. Nor is self-sacrifice and fellow-feeling so entirely the property of a brother but that a father may have full share in them.

And so we find in the Bible the names and titles of the Father and the Son interchanged, and no function is ascribed to the one Divine Person in which the other has no share.

The marriage union which doubles personal life in this world, setting beside the earthly person a subject personality in which it is reflected and repeated, finds its counterpart in the divine sphere. For there are few images more frequently used in the New Testament than that by which the Church, which represents Christ on earth and is the channel of His work and of His authority, is called His bride.

The mysterious and incomprehensible communion between soul and soul in man takes place by outward and visible means, and through the same outward world the self meets its fellow self; though how it does so must ever remain a mystery. And so it is that the sacramental system of Christianity makes earthly and visible things the means whereby the personality of man is brought into communion with that of God. The more we reflect upon the Christian theology the more we feel how consonant it is with life, and that there is nothing of what is best and highest in personal communion and personal consciousness which does not find its completion and the satisfaction of the desires it excites in this holy faith. Human affections, and the habits into which life irresistibly moulds us, are futile and objectless in their best parts, unless they are meant to train us for this eternal communion. We learn in this world to reverence, trust, and love, only to see the objects of these feelings prove unworthy or disappear. And after the long education through pleasure and through pain, which life imparts to us, just when our minds seem capable of some higher and better use than any which has hitherto been afforded them, we ourselves die. A miserable history of waste and disappointment unless we can hope for a renewal of life amidst better and more satisfying conditions, and find an object for the powers of communion of which our personal soul is capable that shall be more complete and lasting than those with which our senses have to do.

87. The wonderful fitness of the Christian creed to satisfy all the wants to which our personal life trains us is a witness to its truth, and of the most persuasive nature; a witness of truth such as we

But its origin was found not in human wants but in revealed facts.

possess for the realities that meet us in life and for their adaptation to our needs. Of these it may be said that they are their own evidence. They do not require to be argued out. And we are conscious that if we attempted to argue upon them we should be entering upon difficult and uncertain questions. Our minds are not able to reproduce the feelings on the strength of which the evidence depends. And we find by experience that our best course is to train and restrain our feelings as well as we can, and when this has been done, to listen to their dictates without over-much questioning. It is on this principle that we choose our friends and the objects of our pursuits in life. Sometimes we make mistakes; but we do so not because we attend to our feelings, but because we leave our feelings untrained. Greater mistakes are made in daily life through not listening to the feelings than through perversions of them. And on the same principle it seems we should choose our religion. No higher proof of the divine origin of a religion can be conceived than an adaptation to satisfy in the greatest degree all the truest wants of human nature; to lay hold of it by that personal quality in which all affections and powers have their centre and so command the whole man. And if we feel unwilling to trust our own consciousness in the matter, we find the proper supplement to our experience and the supply of its deficiencies in the wide acceptance and proved power of this religion among immense numbers and varieties of the highest and best persons and races of men. We cannot be unsafe if we submit ourselves to its happy dominion.

But as the intellect is fertile in doubts, and sometimes demands to be listened to, even when it is opposing what our healthiest impulses require, it is possible that an argument against the divine origin of the Catholic faith might be founded upon that very fitness to human life on which we have been treating. It may be urged that the existence of the want has originated the imagination of its supply, and that just because men have wanted so much better fathers and brothers and selves than they were possessed of, they have invented a Father, Son, and Holy Ghost above this imperfect world. If we were to listen to doubts of this nature we never should believe anything beyond what we see; for that which is ill-fitted to our wants and feelings would be rejected because it is so: and that which is well-fitted to them would be rejected as being too good to be true, and bearing the marks of invention in its very perfection. However, the history of the Christian creed dissipates the doubt. It was not devised by ingenious persons, nor did it come upon the world as a formal system. It grew stage by stage on the basis of facts experienced in the history of a nation and of individuals. And those who deduced the great system from these data had no intention in their minds except that of being true to the revelation which they had received. The wondrous comprehensiveness of the creed which resulted from their labours is due not to them but to the divine author of the revealed facts on which it was founded. Just so the symmetry and completeness of a scientific theory may lead one at first sight to suspect that it is ingeniously framed to meet the intellectual tendencies of the lovers of system. But should it prove to be founded upon the most rigorous observation of facts, we no longer see in its symmetry any sign of human device, but the reflection of a law which proceeds from the mind of the Author of nature. And the same is true of the Christian creed. The mysterious personality of God is deduced from experience, just as that of man: and after all is known that can be known of It, It remains like the personality of man, a mystery still. But it is a mystery which is sufficiently known to explain all life and satisfy every need of the soul of man.

We are not capable of proving beyond dispute any of the more comprehensive truths of human life. Neither our own existence nor the existence of other men, nor the existence of nature, are so demonstrated that an unlimited and unrestrained willingness to doubt them can be crushed by the weight of their evidence. But the question comes at last to this: Does the faith work? Does it bring belief and practice into harmony?. Does it furnish a spiritual equipment fit for life? Does it reconcile experiences that without it are contradictory? And if it does this we accept it. We listen with great indifference to those who would deprive us of it, putting nothing in its place. Now we claim all this for the Catholic faith. It is Catholic in this highest sense that every man can find in it room to exercise in a supreme degree those various powers of body, mind, and soul, with which God endows him, and in which experience educates him. He is provided with adequate objects for that conscious life and that sense of personality which is otherwise, with all its splendour, an anomaly in nature and a misery to himself.

No man need imagine that he is sacrificing truth because he allows conscience and feeling as well as logic room to work in his belief. We opened our subject by laying down that logic is not the only organ for discovering reality, and that feeling as well as intellect is a guide to the truth which surrounds us. It has been further shewn that our deepest feelings are those which are the utterance of our personality claiming free exercise for its own energies and seeking communion with personalities like itself. No systems can be furnishing to man the best truths he is capable of realising if they tend to obscure personality or to deprive him of the faith which can best develop it. And of faiths, the best form will be that which, coming with good warrant from historic fact, enlists our various powers of intellect, conscience and taste, of art and science and speculation, in the freest and fullest exercise under the supreme command of the personal life and will. It will teach us the worth of our personality by what it shews us of our past origin and our future prospects. And it will uplift our personality by the aid which can only come through a real and living union with the Perfect Life of Him who is human and divine, and in Him with all that is best in men past and present; above all, with the eternal being of God.

www.ingramcontent.com/pod-product-compliance
Lightning Source LLC
Chambersburg PA
CBHW032148230426
43672CB00011B/2491